Blood on the Out-Basket

Lessons in Leadership from a Newspaper Junkie

BY MIKE WALLER

KANSAS CITY STAR
BOOKS

Blood on the Out-Basket:
Lessons in Leadership from a Newspaper Junkie

By Mike Waller
mikeewaller@aol.com

Designed by Amy Robertson

Published by Kansas City Star Books
1729 Grand Blvd.
Kansas City, Missouri 64108
All rights reserved.
Copyright© 2011 by Mike Waller

First edition, first printing
ISBN: 978-1-611690-04-0
Library of Congress Control Number: 2011922665

Printed in the United States.

To order copies, call StarInfo at 816-234-4636 and say "operator."

www.TheKansasCityStore.com

KANSAS CITY STAR
BOOKS

Mike Waller in his office while
he was editor of The Kansas City Star
and Times, circa 1983.
Photo courtesy of The Kansas City Star

Contents

Prologue: Blood on the Out-Basket...9

Chapter 1: Share Power 13

Chapter 2: Pursue Excellence 25

Leadership Sketch #1:
Mary Junck, CEO of Lee Enterprises, Inc. 30

Chapter 3: Include Employees................................33

Chapter 4: Respect People..39

Leadership Sketch #2:
Freeman A. Hrabowski III, president,
University of Maryland Baltimore County..........................42

Chapter 5: Champion Teamwork 45

Chapter 6: Be an Agent of Change 57

Leadership Sketch #3:
Marty Petty, CEO, Creative Loafing, Inc. 62

Chapter 7: Excel as an Apostle of Hope 65

Chapter 8: Be a Slave to Integrity 71

Leadership Sketch #4:
Mike Mulvain, owner, Mulvain Woodworks.........................74

Chapter 9: Communicate, Communicate, Communicate 77

Chapter 10: Teach and Coach...81

Leadership Sketch #5:
John S. Carroll, former editor, *The Los Angeles Times* 90

Chapter 11: Listen, Really Listen 93

Chapter 12: Embrace Innovation 95

Leadership Sketch #6:
Hilary Schneider, former executive vice president,
Yahoo! Americas..104

Chapter 13: Commit to Diversity 107

Chapter 14: Take Risks 111

Leadership Sketch #7:
Douglas E. Zemke, former president, Millikin University... 116

Chapter 15: Uphold Standards and Reward Performance 119

Chapter 16: Be Tenacious 123

Leadership Sketch #8:
   Carla D. Hayden, executive director,
   Enoch Pratt Free Library 130

Chapter 17: The Enemies of Leadership 133

Acknowledgements 137

Notes 139

About the Author 145

Prologue:
Blood on the Out-Basket

It was a spring weekday morning in 1979, barely six months after I joined *The Kansas City Star's* staff as managing editor. I arrived at my desk in the newsroom (for nearly 100 years there were no offices in the Star's newsroom) at the usual time of 6:15 a.m., a necessary early hour to begin the process of editing an afternoon newspaper.

The newsroom was nearly empty. Only Dean Evans, the assistant wire editor, and Mike Zakoura, an assistant city editor, were at their posts. My desk was directly behind Zakoura's and in front of the south wall's small conference room, built after Capital Cities Communications had acquired in 1977 the Star and Times for $126 million, a then-record amount for the purchase of a newspaper.

Across an aisle on my right were the desks of George Burg, a former Star managing editor who was the assistant to the publisher, and his secretary, Grace Grafton.

As usual, I busied myself reading the morning editions of *The Kansas City Times,* The Star's sister paper. Shortly before 7 a.m., as she did everyday, Grace appeared in the entrance to the newsroom and headed toward her desk. After hanging her coat on a rack behind her desk, Grace sat down. Suddenly, she leaped to her feet and screamed: "There's blood on the out-basket!"

I jumped up and immediately shouted: "That's the name of my book."

Upon inspection, we indeed did discover blood on Grace's out-basket. Further reporting revealed that earlier that morning a couple of pressman had wandered into the newsroom and wound up in a knife fight, leaving their red signature on her out-basket.

Over the years I often thought about writing a book about my newspaper experiences. Thirty-two years later, here it is, a book that focuses on leadership principles using my experiences as an editor and publisher as illustrations and entitled "Blood on the Out-Basket: Lessons in Leadership From a News-paper Junkie."

Readers rightfully may wonder what my credentials are for giving advice about leadership.

I have 41 years experience in the newspaper business, 30 years as a senior editor or CEO and publisher. I was the only editor in the history of *The Kansas City Star and Times* to hold all three of the highest editing positions: managing editor of The Star, managing editor of The Times and editor of The Star and Times. I also was executive editor and editor of *The Hartford Courant* before becoming the paper's publisher and CEO in 1994. I retired at the end of 2002 after five years as publisher and CEO of *The Sun* in Baltimore.

During my years there, The Courant employed about 1,500 people and had sales of more than $200 million while *The Sun* employed about 1,800 people with sales of more than $350 million. As the top editor, I managed budgets of $10 million to $20 million and led staffs ranging in size from 350 to 385 journalists. During my career, the newspapers I worked on won dozens of national awards, including eight Pulitzer Prizes. As the publisher in Hartford and Baltimore, I was chairman of United Way campaigns that jointly raised about $70 million. I also taught more than 1,200 managers attending leadership classes at the Times Mirror Leadership Institute for Managers from its inception in 1994 to its demise in 2000 with the acquisition of Times Mirror by Tribune Co. During that time I became even more convinced that the most effective leadership included the sharing of power with employees, encouraging teamwork, communicating well and often, teaching and being an agent of change and an apostle of hope, all aimed at inspiring people to do their best work.

Some readers may wonder why anyone should take advice from someone in an industry that has fallen out of favor and is in decline. The answer is simple: These leadership principles worked well when newspapers were earning gobs of money and they work well today for leaders in many different kinds of successful businesses. They'll work well for you, too, if you follow them faithfully.

CHAPTER 1:
Share Power

*"Give people the vision and hold them accountable,
but let them do it their own way.
They'll be more fulfilled and the work will be better."*
—KURT SCHNEIDER, CEO OF THE HARLEM GLOBETROTTERS

By many accounts, mostly in *The Wall Street Journal,* Stan O'Neal was a man to admire. The CEO of Merrill Lynch & Co. was smart, immensely talented and driven. Over the years he was credited with increasing the company's profitability and transforming it from an American-focused broker to an international financial giant with strong positions in such important financial segments as commodities, asset management and bonds.

Overcoming a childhood of poverty in the Deep South, O'Neal worked at General Motors before joining Merrill Lynch in 1986. By 2002, he advanced to the head of the class at Merrill Lynch.

Yet in October 2007, under O'Neal's leadership, Merrill Lynch announced a write-down of $8.4 billion in the third quarter, $7.9 billion of it connected to its revaluation of mortgage-related assets—the biggest loss in Wall Street memory.

Just as astonishing to many Wall Street executives was the swiftness with which Merrill's board of directors, most of whom were hand-picked by O'Neal, kicked him out.

At first glance, O'Neal's downfall seemed a simple conse-
quence of a historic financial failure. But a closer look, according to several former colleagues, revealed a tragic flaw: O'Neal
didn't know how to share power. He rarely engaged in debate,
kept his own counsel and had little use for strong-willed subordinates who might have helped him avoid the subprime mort-
gage disaster that toppled him.

"He was uncomfortable around independent people (with)
views that might be different than his, and whose loyalty was to
the firm rather than to him personally," Barry Friedberg, Merrill Lynch's longtime head of investment banking, was quoted
in *The Wall Street Journal.*

In addition, O'Neal was a flawed communicator. He reported
to the board in late September that Merrill Lynch expected a
$4.5 billion write-down. But less than a month later the write-
down was announced at $8.4 billion. Wall Street Journal sourc-
es said O'Neal didn't explain to the board as well as he should
have the reasons for such a large increase in losses in such a
short period of time.

There are many lessons in the O'Neal tragedy. Perhaps the
most important one is for leaders to learn how to share power.

A leader's first job is to inspire employees to do their best
work, clear hurdles out of their way and seize his excitement
and satisfaction through the success of others. This cannot be
achieved over a sustained period of without sharing power.

Gordon M. Bethune, former CEO of Continental Airlines, put
it this way in an interview in *The New York Times:*

"The really good people want autonomy—you let me do it
and I'll do it. So I told the people I recruited: 'You come in here
and you've got to keep me informed, but you're the guy, and
you'll make these decisions. It won't be me second-guessing
you. But everybody's going to win together. We're part of a
team, but you're going to run your part.' That's all they want.
They want a chance to do it."

Much of life, from the time we are toddlers, is filled with skirmishes about power and turf. Consider any recent disputes you have had at your workplace. More often than not, the argument was not about the topic in question but rather about an effort to retain or gain power.

Information is power, and that's why many managers love to hoard it. If they know something you don't know, they have a slice of power that you lack. That's why it is difficult to get managers to share information. In fact, except for proprietary information, most of the information known by top managers could be shared with all employees.

Sources quoted in *The New York Times* contend that Rahm Emanuel, former chief of staff for President Obama, believes the more someone uses power the more power he accumulates. My experience suggests just the opposite, as outlined in what I call the **Trinity of Power:**

• **The more you use it the more you lose it.** So choose carefully when to exercise power.

• **The source of power is people, not position.** Power is granted to you by those who work for you, not by those for whom you work. Your title will only carry you so far.

• **Power flows in the direction of hope.** Your job is to prevent powerlessness, which produces despair, stifles enthusiasm and saps energy. Put everyone in charge of something. You can share power and knowledge and wind up being more powerful than ever.

Most newspapers, and many other companies, are top-down organizations in which most of the more significant decisions are made by a handful of people, usually an executive committee and/or a committee of senior managers.

That was the structure of *The Hartford Courant,* similar to nearly all metropolitan newspapers, when I was promoted to publisher and CEO of the newspaper in 1994 after eight years as executive editor and editor.

The executive committee consisted of the publisher, the general manager, the chief financial officer, the editor and the editor of the editorial pages. It met each morning and made nearly all of the significant business decisions of the company. News and editorial decisions were left to the appropriate editors.

But that system severely underutilized our brain power and left most managers in charge of very little.

I, and our general manager, Marty Petty, believed that people want to get better at what they do, that they want to have some choice in what they do and how they do it, and that they want to feel they are contributing. We also believed that much more information about the company could be shared with far more people. And we thought The Courant was a great place to try a different leadership model: it had no unions with stifling work rules and had operated over the years as if it were one great big family.

In 1995, Times Mirror, The Courant's parent company, hired a new CEO—Mark Willes—whose early instructions called for all the TM newspapers to significantly reduce costs and increase profitability. Thus into our vocabulary leapt the word "downsizing" and we initiated The Courant's first employee buyouts—the oldest, continuously published newspaper in America had never bought out or laid off an employee since its founding in 1764, even during The Depression.

We took several months to execute the buyout plan, which kept all the senior managers extremely busy, delaying our revamping of the leadership structure.

But by mid-1995 we began the difficult task of creating a new leadership model based on the sharing of power. The senior managers, conferring with many middle managers, met in retreats and in dozens of other meetings, hashing over the new model. We created the structure from scratch; we were aware of no other model meeting our goals that we could adopt.

The goals, easier to fashion than the actual leadership structure, included:

- Facilitating communication.
- Putting decision-making into the hands of the many instead of the few, delegating to one another many company decisions and trusting in the result, even if we might have personally chosen another path.
- Providing opportunities for personal growth and development.
- Challenging all of us to reach beyond our expectations.
- Building teams of key departmental leaders focused on the paper's mission, vision and values.
- Changing how we lead, sharing power with all our associates and promoting innovative change throughout the company.
- Investing in all forms of education for our staffs.
- Serving customers better and faster.

After all the senior managers signed off on the realignment, the new structure was unveiled in May 1996. It demanded that The Courant focus on its business priorities through eight Leadership Committees: Innovation, Operating, Strategic Planning, Staff Development and Leadership, Workplace, Business Development and Acquisition, Technology, and Readership. Eventually a committee on Civic Responsibility was added.

Each consisted of a chair, a vice chair and six or seven members, chosen by me in consultation with all the senior managers from the top 90 managers in the newspaper. Senior managers became members of two committees. The chairs and vice chairs were given special training on how to conduct effective meetings.

The committees dealt with cross-departmental issues only; they were not authorized to interfere with departmental authority. The committees were charged with making decisions, keeping me, Marty and the other leaders informed along the way. I reserved the right to veto a decision, but vowed to use the veto sparingly.

From the beginning, the committees were to issue regular reports about their various activities to all managers, but the communications were spotty. Committee reports were often far too long and not always issued in a timely fashion. We formed a small Communications Oversight Committee that soon had communications flowing smoothly. But it wasn't long before many managers felt overwhelmed by all the information and believed there was too much communication.

I kept my Times Mirror supervisor, Don Wright, generally informed about the new model but without offering a lot of detail. I knew he would love the idea of sharing power, and he did.

About six months after the unveiling of the new leadership model, I asked John Zakarian, editor of the editorial board and a member of the Staff Development and Leadership Committee, to chronicle the transformation through interviews with the leaders, personal observations and an examination of the raw data. Zakarian's report included these highlights:

"The work got off to a slow start. In the first two months, committees often made recommendations instead of decisions. Some members didn't really believe they had the authority to make decisions. But soon more and more decisions were being made without permission from the top. However, not enough of the decisions were being pushed down into the middle management. The effectiveness of the committees was directly related to the skill of the chair and could be measured by the results. All of the committees achieved many excellent results, some more easily than others. Within each committee, work relationships improved. Some senior managers found it challenging to do their departmental work as well as their committee work. Two of them reduced their membership to one committee."

I found myself more isolated than I had been under the old leadership structure and not as well informed about daily operations. So I simply used my reporting experience and spent more time in each of the departments and with the committee leaders asking lots of questions. It was more work, but more rewarding, too.

One drawback of the model was the overlap and occasional friction between a committee and the department with similar responsibilities. Elaine Kramer, a former Courant news editor and at the time the assistant to the publisher, cited as an example the Workplace Committee and the Human Resources Department. "Often the work of the committee rubbed up against the work of the HR Department," she says. "Sometimes the two groups' initiatives complimented each other but other times they conflicted. This caused some confusion and some resentment."

But the problem of jurisdictional overlap among the committees and departments nearly always got resolved by the participants themselves.

One example of overlap occurred when the Operating Committee became actively involved in decisions on the newspaper's sponsorship and handling of the U.S. presidential debate in Hartford in 1996.

The Operating Committee wanted to make speedy decisions on various matters, including printing an Extra edition immediately after the debate. But the editor, co-chair of the Readership Committee, was balking. Yet even in this sensitive jurisdictional overlap there was no stalemate. The leaders of each group ironed out their differences well in advance of the debate and the result was that The Courant's coverage won widespread acclaim, the paper added $100,000 in incremental advertising and The Courant's community involvement was widely praised.

Most of the committee members thoroughly enjoyed their new responsibilities even though it forced them into more work—they still had to do their regular jobs. But they loved having a voice in the operation of the company.

Lou Golden, a former Courant business editor who had become the vice president of marketing, remembers it this way:

"The Leadership Model increased the flow of information throughout the company. The monthly operational report we prepared for Times Mirror was disseminated to all managers and later to all employees, omitting only the most highly sensitive or competitive information. If managers were going to guide the company, they needed the operational data to do it.

"In many ways the model was successful. It leveled the pyramid of power. Many managers suddenly were involved in, and caring about, areas of the company they knew little about. It also broke down the silos of each department and increased managers' understanding of companywide issues.

"It also helped foster relationships within the management throughout the company, perhaps its greatest achievement. And in many cases, it led to good decisions—I remember that the move to make Martin Luther King Jr. Day a paid holiday came via the Workplace Committee.

"However, it was threatening to some top managers, in particular those who did not understand how to share power. Those who depended on the authority of their positions rather than the authority of their leadership clung to old habits."

The newsroom, a body historically independent from the business departments, tolerated the model more than embraced it.

David Fink, the politics and government editor, explained it this way:

"News managers were more skeptical than others about the model and about taking part in it. For one thing, news people are anarchists, not joiners. Beyond that, this was one of the first and definitely the most organized integration of News and the Business Side most had ever seen. They weren't sure how it would work or if it should work.

"But it did work, mainly because people trusted you (and Marty). You had built up capital, which is saying something in a newsroom, and so a lot of people went along."

Because most of the news managers went along, managers in other departments who might have been reluctant but were aware of the historic independence of and resistance to change in the newsroom quickly joined the effort, figuring that if the news folks could do it surely they could, too. Kramer and most other middle managers found the work invigorating.

"I found it tremendously valuable, as a Workplace Committee member, to learn about an area of our business that normally would have been well outside my job purview. There was a constant foment of ideas, and rich discussions about policies, practices, initiatives and workplace benefits.

"I particularly remember a discussion about vacation policies—should we change the pace at which employees earned vacation time? Everyone liked the idea for more vacation for all, but recognized that any liberalization would come at a cost. The main question was: would an increase in vacation time bring measurable results in improved morale?

"The committee identified what the cost would be, but then discussed what else might be done with that money that might improve workplace conditions even more."

In the end, the committee did not elect to increase vacation time or spend the money on other workplace issues, proving a theory I had had for years: If you give smart people the same information you have, they most often will make the same decision you would have made. And sometimes, they will make a different decision from what you would have made, and time would prove it to be a better one than yours.

At the end of the first year, we published a brochure listing the committees' achievements, which totaled 105. A few examples of the major ones were:

- Expanding the printing of the editions of the weekly

BLOOD ON THE OUT-BASKET

newspaper The Advocate (Business Development and Acquisitions Committee).

• Coordinating special sections targeted to the advancement of the New England Patriots in the Super Bowl that resulted in increased advertising sales of nearly $30,000 (Operations and Readership committees).

• Expanding local news, arts and sports coverage in response to a new startup of a competitive Sunday paper and redesigning the entire newspaper (Readership Committee).

• Developing the 1997-1999 strategic plan and aligning the goals of the senior managers to it (Strategic Planning).

• Revising and distributing a new Employee Handbook and developing and instituting a new mileage reimbursement policy (Workplace Committee).

In October 1997, I was named publisher of Times Mirror's Baltimore Sun and Marty Petty replaced me as publisher of The Courant. She continued to adjust the Leadership Model, constantly rotating membership and chairs on the committees and devising more effective ways to engage all the managers.

The Tribune Co. merged with Times-Mirror in June 2000. Shortly afterward, Marty joined *The St. Petersburg Times* as general manager and Tribune named Jack Davis publisher of The Courant.

It took Tribune and Davis only a few weeks to abandon the Leadership Model and revert to the top-down structure of an executive committee and senior management committee, putting decision-making back into the hands of the few.

In truth, it's doubtful that few if any other publishers in America would have bought in to the model of sharing power. Nearly all of them grew up in and were comfortable with the top-down structure.

A few years after we instituted the model, I was told by a Times Mirror source that the TM chairman and president, Willes and Dick Schlosberg, thought I had lost my mind when they learned of our adoption of the new leadership structure. But to their credit, they never interfered and not once ever mentioned their doubts to me. In effect, they chose to share their power with me. Of course, it didn't hurt that The Courant posted double-digit revenue and profitability gains throughout the early years of the new model.

Would all of the good decisions and successes accomplished under the model have been the same under the old-top-down leadership structure? Many, perhaps most, would have been achieved. But most of the decisions would have been made by four or five top leaders, not by 90 newly empowered key managers. And there would have been no explosion of soaring morale among the managers without the power-sharing model.

The Leadership Model reinforced my belief that the sharing of power, no matter how it is done, is the No. 1 attribute in being a good leader.

How You Can Share Power: You don't have to be a CEO to share power. Anyone in a leadership position can do it. It's simply a matter of delegating authority to those you supervise and allowing them to make decisions that you previously might have made yourself. It's important that you prepare them for decision-making, through formal and informal training. Once you delegate your power, do your best not to second-guess their decision. Remember that there are many right ways to do things. You can always veto a decision if necessary. But the more you use your veto the less employees are empowered and the more you undercut yourself. Enlightened companies are eliminating the command-and-control leadership model. If you work for an unenlightened company, you can still share power with employees by creating opportunities for everyone in your group to be in charge of something and have a chance to shine.

CHAPTER 2:
Pursue Excellence

"Perfection is not obtainable,
but if we chase perfection we can catch excellence."

—VINCE LOMBARDI, FORMER COACH, GREEN BAY PACKERS

The Greek philosophers contended that people should pursue excellence, not happiness. They believed that the pursuit of excellence would lead to happiness. I found that to be true in the newspaper business.

When I began my newspaper career in 1961, I believed newspapers were in the business of pursuing excellence. I discovered later, much to my dismay, that pursuing excellence was not even on the list of most newspapers. Pursuing profits was; it headed the list.

But some newspapers were dedicated to finding excellence. Only six years after entering the business, I was fortunate to work at one—*The Courier-Journal* in Louisville, Ky. (I later worked at four others—*The Louisville Times,* sister paper of *The Courier-Journal, The Kansas City Star and Times,* owned by Capital Cities, Inc., and *The Hartford Courant* and *The Sun* in Baltimore, owned by Times Mirror Co.).

Owned by the Bingham family, *The Courier-Journal* was obsessed with producing a high quality newspaper every day. It was the mantra of all newsroom leaders and became the by-word of the entire newsroom, from reporters and copy editors to photographers and artists.

As a copy editor on the copy desk, I and several of my colleagues vowed each night to have a perfect record and make no mistakes in editing the stories assigned to us. Alas, the chief of the copy desk always found an error or two and we never reached our goal.

Each night a copy editor and an editor on the city desk were assigned to the late shift, staying until about 2 a.m. reading page proofs (copies of newspaper pages), rechecking all the stories for any errors. If an error was found, no matter how small—a misplaced comma, perhaps—the type was corrected and the page was put back on the press for the remaining copies yet to be printed. It was a costly procedure—sending back one page cost a few dollars. But excellence was important—we sent back dozens of pages every night. Few, if any, newspapers bother anymore.

Excellence also was a goal in all that we did during my tenure at *The Hartford Courant.* Shortly after I arrived in 1986 as executive editor, the company adopted a mission and vision statement that emphasized the pursuit of excellence. It read, in part:

"The Hartford Courant is committed to providing the information Connecticut needs and to being a responsible force for progress in our community...in fulfilling this mission, we will maintain the highest standards of ethics, accuracy, fairness, service and timeliness."The vision statement read: "Customers can depend on all of us to deliver our best every day."

The news department created it own mission statement: "The Hartford Courant seeks to provide the news Connecticut needs, reported faithfully and fully, with respect for all and favor to none...." The first goal listed was: "To be the indispensable, timely source of information on the economic, political, social, sporting and cultural life of Connecticut; and in that pursuit to excel at community coverage, examining all local subjects that touch readers."

In both Louisville and Hartford, the owners provided the necessary funds—far more than most papers of similar circulation size—to reach for excellence. And most employees at each paper paid more than casual attention to the mission statements.

Another great believer in high quality content was Richard E. Deems, longtime president of the magazine division of Hearst Corp. who helped revive two storied magazines, *Cosmopolitan* and *Good Housekeeping*. He pursued excellence even in difficult financial times, believing that all you had to do was "just get the best thing on the page and the economy will take care of itself."

One of the best examples of pursuing excellence I ever encountered was at the University of Maryland in Baltimore County (UMBC).

In 1988, the provost at UMBC, Dr. Freeman Hrabowski, was introduced to Robert and Jane Meyerhoff, prominent Baltimore civic leaders who had a vision of a minority-oriented achievement program. Dr. Hrabowski, who graduated at age 19 from Hampton Institute with the highest honors in mathematics, believed that UMBC could provide a supportive learning environment for talented students of color in science, mathematics, engineering and related fields.

In what was considered a bold experiment at the time, the Meyerhoffs provided the funding for a scholarship program to prepare young African-American men committed to earning Ph.D degrees for careers in scientific research. The first class in 1989 attracted 19 students and a year later the first women were admitted to the program.

The program was so successful that by 1996 UMBC was honored with the Presidential Award for Excellence for Science, Mathematics and Engineering Mentoring from President Bill Clinton.

Since 1993, the Meyerhoff Scholarship program has graduated more than 600 students of color. As of 2008, 53 have earned Ph.D degrees, 21 have earned M.D./Ph.D degrees, 74 have earned M.D. degrees and 115 have earned M.S. degrees from America's greatest universities, including Harvard, Yale, Stanford, Duke, Pennsylvania, Johns Hopkins and Carnegie Mellon. In addition, 250 Meyerhoff alumni are enrolled in graduate and professional schools.

Dr. Hrabowski, who has been president of UMBC since 1992 and was named in 2009 by Time Magazine as one of the nation's top 10 college presidents, has been dedicated to pursuing excellence in other ways. Under his leadership, UMBC was named in 2009 the No. 1 "up-and-coming" national university in the college rankings by U.S. News & World Report Magazine. U.S. News also named UMBC No. 4, tied with Stanford, on a list of national universities most committed to teaching undergraduates.

The workplace proverb "if it's worth doing, it's worth doing right" still holds true. Yet fewer and fewer companies and organizations live by that today.

How You Can Pursue Excellence: Remember when you were an adolescent playing competitive sports or trying to make the honor roll in high school or working in your first part-time job bagging groceries? Most likely you were always pushing yourself to get better. You might not have realized it at the time but that's pursuing excellence. The key is to take small steps, trying to outdo yesterday and always reaching higher. Small steps over time add up to significant improvement.

Mary Junck
chairman, president and CEO
of Lee Enterprises, Inc.

Leadership Sketch No. 1

Mary Junck joined Lee Enterprises, which owns 49 daily newspapers and more than 300 weekly newspapers and specialty publications in 23 states, in 1999. She is a member of the board of directors of The Associated Press and a former board member of the Newspaper Association of America.

Before joining Lee, Mary was executive vice president of Times Mirror and president of Times Mirror Eastern Newspapers, overseeing the operations of Newsday, The Sun in Baltimore, The Hartford Courant, The Morning Call in Allentown, Pa., and Southern Connecticut Newspapers in Stamford and Greenwich. From 1993 to 1997 she was publisher and CEO of The Sun, moving from St. Paul, Minn., where she was publisher and president of The Pioneer Press. She also held executive positions at The Charlotte Observer, The Miami Herald and on the Knight Ridder corporate staff.

In St. Paul, Baltimore and Davenport, Mary was a member of more than a dozen civic boards, including The Greater Baltimore Alliance, the Baltimore Symphony Orchestra and Quad Cities First.

She is a native of Ogden, Iowa, and earned a bachelor of arts degree in English at Valparaiso University in Indiana and a master's degree in journalism at the University of North Carolina at Chapel Hill.

Mary's key leadership tips are:

- **Be positive, optimistic and enthusiastic.** My favorite quote on the importance of enthusiasm is from Ralph Waldo Emerson: "Nothing great was ever achieved without enthusiasm." You should aim to be positive, optimistic and enthusiastic every day—even if things aren't going your way.

- **Really listen.** Listening means shutting your mouth and really listening to what others (employees, customers, team members, vendors) are saying about your company and your products. Almost without fail, the solutions to business challengers as well as innovative ideas are found by listening.

- **Get things done.** Many unsuccessful leaders fail because they are poor at execution—they don't get things done, are indecisive and don't deliver on commitments. Be someone who is disciplined, takes action and gets things done.

- **Be nice.** Although business can be rough and tumble, a crucial leadership trait is empathy and kindness. Maybe your mother advised you: "It's nice to be important, but it's more important to be nice." Here's more: Treat others with respect, send congratulatory notes, smile. Everyone loves praise—look hard for ways to give it.

CHAPTER 3:

Include Employees

"None of us is as smart as all of us."

—OLD JAPANESE PROVERB

Not only do leaders too often resist sharing power with subordinates, most companies rarely tap into the vast brainpower of their employees.

A survey done more than a decade ago by consultant Kepner-Trogue Inc., in Princeton, N. J. found that nearly two-thirds of the 641 managers and 773 hourly workers interviewed believed their companies didn't use more than half their employees' brainpower. Worse yet, more than 70 per cent compared their organizations to a slow-moving truck or a ho-hum car, blaming failure to involve employees in decisions and lack of training or rewards.

Inclusion is a powerful tool for leaders. I found out early in my career that no matter how brilliant and experienced the top person was, the collective wisdom of the staff is nearly always greater. Leaders should create an atmosphere is which disagreement is welcome and everyone's ideas are heard, even though some ideas are better than others.

I experienced the power of inclusion when George Bahamonde, the president and CEO of the United Way of the Capital

Area in Hartford, asked me to be the chairman of the 1997 campaign. I accepted, provided the Cabinet (the voluntary chairs of the 30 or so employee fund-raising divisions) had a voice in determining the financial goal of the campaign.

Usually, the final goal of the campaign was decided by the campaign chair, the president and a few other key staff members after studying the data from all the divisions the previous year. The Cabinet was then informed of the goal.

Bahamonde, a Cuban who came to America unable to speak English, had an uncanny ability to connect with people. He was as comfortable in a soup kitchen as in a corporate suite and headed the Hartford United Way for 12 years before he died in July 2006.

He and I and other United Way staff members analyzed the 1996 fund-raising data and thought the goal should be $20 million, a slight increase over the previous year. We then held our first meeting of the Cabinet, about 30 business executives chairing the divisions, ranging from Major Corporate and United Technology Corp. (a division by itself) to Government and Non-Profit Organizations. We provided all the division chairs with the 1996 data in advance and asked them to report at the meeting how much they thought their division could raise in 1977. One by one, the chairs listed their goals on a blackboard. When totaled, the sum added up to about $20 million, the same figure we had privately reached.

And then the chairs did something remarkable. They decided on their own that they wanted to have a second, private goal. Once again, the chairs stood up and explained how they would raise more money.

The second goal added nearly $500,000 to the $20 million, which became the publicly announced goal. In September, I left for my new position as the publisher of The Sun and Ron Copes, an executive with Massachusetts General, replaced me as chair of the campaign. When the campaign ended in November, it surpassed both the public goal and the private goal and raised a total of nearly $21 million, a record amount at the time.

The results can be just the opposite when employees aren't included.

When I arrived at *The Sun* in the fall of 1997, the Circulation Department was in the middle stage of converting the distribution of the newspaper to a new system. Previously, the paper was delivered to subscribers by hundreds of carriers paid under an individually negotiated contract.

Responding to a company request to reduce expenses, the Circulation Vice President recommended that *The Sun* convert in three stages over a few months to a system of about 70 "mega-route" distributors, who would be paid more than the previous carriers. But since there were fewer carriers the total cost would be less. He estimated the savings would be $2 million a year and believed that customer service would improve.

My first experience with The Sun's budget came when the September numbers were compiled in early October. The Circulation Department showed no savings. Instead, the department's expenses were a half-million dollars over budget even after extra funds had been added for the conversion.

The Circulation Vice President assured me that the September number was a one-time blip.

At the same time, readers began calling my office complaining about late or non-delivery of their newspapers. A couple of complaints a week were normal. Within a matter of weeks, I was getting about 20 complaints a day. The Circulation Department, it turned out, was getting hundreds a day.

In early November, the October budget figures arrived. The Circulation Department was another half-million dollars over budget. Worse, the delivery complaints had exploded and cancellations mounted.

I asked a key financial executive, Rich Goldstein, and two other financial assistants to conduct an investigation to determine what had gone wrong and recommend any course corrections.

Goldstein's team discovered several flaws in the conversion. Among them:

- There were dozens of unforeseen delivery problems, many caused by our antiquated technology system. We had made huge changes in the distribution of the newspaper but didn't install any updated technology to support them.
- In an effort to offset the circulation losses, we instituted large discounts to attract new subscribers and keep the old ones from canceling. This led to much less revenue than budgeted.
- We lost some of our best distributors because they realized their territories were too large to properly serve customers. To offset the losses, we increased our payments to the distributors who stayed and added more to reduce the size of their routes. Thus we increased our expenses and reduced our revenue.

When the dust had settled, we lost several million dollars and 20,000 subscribers in about six months. Because we were having a great financial year, we covered all the cost overruns and still exceeded our profit goals. But we never did recover most of the lost subscribers.

The Circulation Vice President had many good qualities and had an outstanding record at dreaming up good ideas. But as a leader, he had a couple of serious flaws: he was not collaborative, rarely consulting his staff, and he did not tolerate disagreement or bad news. Thus staff members, most of whom did not think the conversion would work, were not consulted and did not volunteer their opinion.

Shortly thereafter we discovered that *Newsday*, another newspaper owned by Times Mirror, had converted to a "mega-route" system. But *Newsday* took several years to do it and upgraded its technology to support the conversion long before it made the switch. We, therefore, could have avoided our disaster simply by discovering the *Newsday* approach, including our employees from the beginning and welcoming disagreement in the workplace.

The entire episode reminded me of another workplace proverb: When in doubt, consult the people closest to the work.

How You Can Include Employees: One of the best ways to include employees is to communicate openly with them. Keeping them informed and sharing information with them will reinforce their importance to the organization. Giving them opportunities to offer ideas, really listening to them and acting on some of the best ideas will generate loyalty and even more ownership in the company.

CHAPTER 4:

Respect People

"You don't lead by hitting people over the head—that's assault, not leadership."

—PRESIDENT DWIGHT D. EISENHOWER

Joe Gibbs won three Super Bowls as head coach of the Washington Redskins and then formed Joe Gibbs Racing in 1991 and proceeded to win 75 NASCAR races and three Sprint Cup championships.

When asked how he keeps more than 400 employees focused on a common goal, Gibbs says that leaders must treat everyone with respect and make everyone feel important. "You want people to understand how much their role matters," he says. "Our drivers and crew chiefs are highly recruited and paid. But the guys who change tires have a crucial role, too. So does our receptionist. For a lot of people, their entire impression of Joe Gibbs Racing is going to be her."

Greg Brenneman, former CEO of Quiznos and Burger Queen, would agree. "The most important thing is that you treat everybody incredibly well and lead with a bit of humility," he says. When he was a consultant with Bain & Company, Brenneman remembers some advice that the CEO, Mitt Romney, told him: "In any interaction, you either gain share or lose share. So treat every interaction as kind of a precious moment in time."

Many leaders who are new to their companies start on the wrong foot by immediately bringing in their own lieutenants and replacing those in the top positions. This shows total disrespect for the managers who were there first and causes hard feelings among the new and old staffs that frequently can't be overcome.

I believed a much more effective approach was to give each senior manager a reasonable chance to succeed and replace only the ones who proved they couldn't get the job done. Over the years, I was forced to make only a few changes in the leadership teams when I moved to a new paper.

Disrespect also rears its ugly head nearly every day at meetings. Many people are late to meetings, sending a message that their time is more important than those who showed up on time. Most meetings last far too long, aren't well organized and are even more poorly run.

At *The Hartford Courant,* we decided to institute Meeting Ground Rules, to assure that all in attendance were treated with respect and that their time was valued. The rules were:

- Be punctual—arrive on time.
- Listen to understand.
- Don't interrupt—let each person fully express an idea.
- No outside interruptions (shut off those cell phones).
- No personal attacks.
- Accept results of group votes.
- Be prepared to participate fully.
- Be sensitive to the feelings and needs of others.
- Everyone has an equal voice.
- All ideas are valuable even though not all are equal.

In addition, we insisted that all meetings have an agenda and start and finish on time. That meant the chair of the meeting had to skillfully lead the session so that the agenda fit the allotted time and the meeting ended promptly. Deadlines were sacred and not to be broken.

Another effective way to convey respect is to lead by "walking around" and "working the room." Leaders should spend as much time as possible chatting with staff members, showing they care about their work and pushing them on to succeed. Many will be inspired by the attention.

Respecting employees also means respecting the company's history. To learn it and honor it sends a message of respect to those who helped shape it.

All the newspapers for which I worked had fabulous histories, none more rich and exciting than The Courant, the oldest continuously published newspaper in America.

The weekly newspaper was founded by Thomas Green in 1764, nearly 25 years before the U.S. Constitution was adopted and took effect. Twelve years after its founding, The Courant printed the full text of the Declaration of Independence.

The Thomas Green Club was a natural outgrowth years later to honor the fourth-generation printer and all Courant employees with 25 years or more service. The Courant invited all the members each year to a dinner at which the company's annual bonus for all employees was announced.

It's no coincidence that many of the leaders profiled in this book's Leadership Sketches mention respecting people as one of the key traits of good leaders.

How You Can Respect People: Leaders respect employees by trusting them, communicating honestly with them, coaching them and celebrating their achievements.

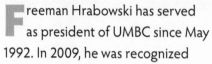

Freeman A. Hrabowski III
president of the University of Maryland, Baltimore County

Leadership Sketch No. 2

Freeman Hrabowski has served as president of UMBC since May 1992. In 2009, he was recognized by Time magazine as one of the nation's top 10 college presidents. A year earlier, Dr. Hrabowski was named one of America's best leaders by U.S. News & World Report, which in 2008 ranked UMBC as the No. 1 "Up and Coming" university in the nation.

His dozens of honors include election to the American Academy of Arts & Sciences and the American Philosophical Society. He serves as a consultant to the National Science Foundation and on many non-profit boards, including the Carnegie Foundation for the Advancement of Teaching, the Alfred P. Sloan Foundation and the France-Merrick Foundation. He also sits on the boards of Constellation Energy Group, McCormick & Company and the Baltimore Equitable Society.

Born in 1950 in Birmingham, Ala., Dr. Hrabowski graduated at age 19 from Hampton Institute with the highest honors in mathematics. At the University of Illinois at Urbana-Champaign, he earned his master's degree in mathematics and his Ph.D four years later, at age 24, in higher education administration/statistics.

A child-leader in the Civil Rights Movement, he was prominently featured in Spike Lee's 1997 documentary, Four Little Girls, on the racially motivated bombing in 1963 of Birmingham's 16th Street Baptist Church.

Dr. Hrabowski has authored numerous articles and co-authored two books, Beating the Odds and Overcoming the Odds, focusing on parenting and high-achieving African-American students in science.

Freeman's key leadership tips are:

- **Authenticity:** No leadership trait is more important than authenticity. It doesn't take long for people to know if a leader is sincere, truly believes what he or she says, and acts consistently with integrity.

- **Building Consensus:** Leaders who have a lasting impact on their organizations understand the importance of constantly asking good questions, of listening carefully, and of building consensus on the organization's vision and strategies for reaching the vision.

- **You Can Never Not Lead:** Leaders should always remember that by what they say—and by what they don't say—they are sending messages that reflect what they really believe, and those messages often shape how others act. Leaders should always be asking the question, "How will others respond to what I say and do?"

- **Humility:** It's very easy for a leader to believe that he or she is more important than he or she really is. In fact, when a leader leaves an organization, it doesn't take long for people to be focused on the new leader and to forget the former. What really matters is the mission and people of the organization.

CHAPTER 5:

Champion Teamwork

"Talent wins games, but teamwork
and intelligence wins championships."

—MICHAEL JORDAN, NBA HALL OF FAMER

One of the great lessons that Brandeis University professor Morrie Schwartz taught Mitch Albom was teamwork. As Morrie lay dying of Lou Gehrig's disease, he told Albom, a columnist for *The Detroit Free Press* and the author of *Tuesdays With Morrie,* the tale of a wave and the ocean in which the little wave suddenly realizes he's going to crash against the shore. He becomes distraught until another wave explains that they're not really waves but are simply part of the ocean.

Morrie's message was clear: Don't be a loner, be part of the team.

Effective teams are like a good basketball squad. A great example is the Oklahoma City Thunder of the NBA. The Thunder and its 30-year old general manager, Sam Presti, had moved from Seattle after the 2007-2008 season. Presti sought hardworking, high-character, low-maintenance athletes who loved to play and sacrificed individual achievements for team success. He traded veterans who didn't fit his vision of team. The results were quick and stunning: The Thunder went from winning only 23 games in 2008- 2009 to 50 of 82 in 2009-2010 and a spot in the playoffs.

The same is true in the workplace. Real team members sacrifice themselves for the good of the team. Teammates play down their own achievements, promote the successes of others and instill confidence in everyone around them. Good teams show self-discipline and hold themselves accountable. By doing so, they build up trust and high standards.

One of the greatest examples of teamwork I ever witnessed was as managing editor of *The Kansas City Star* in the first days after the collapse of the skywalks at the Hyatt Regency Crown Center Hotel on July 17, 1981.

The Star softball team, of which I was a member, had won by a forfeit early that Friday evening and repaired to a bar on the city's northeast side, The Bigger Jigger, to celebrate.

The Star's city editor and his wife, David and Valarie Zeeck, an assistant city editor and his wife, Darryl and Theresa Levings, and a Star reporter and his wife, Rick and Melanie Alm, had just finished dinner at the Hereford House a couple blocks from The Star and about a half-dozen blocks from the Hyatt. As they were leaving about 7:15 p.m. for the Starlight Theater in Swope Park for a concert with Roberta Flack, they encountered two women splattered with blood entering the restaurant and asking to use a public telephone (no cell phones existed then). The editors quizzed the women, who told them the Hyatt had collapsed. Levings quickly gathered notebooks and pens out of his car. The three journalists sent their wives to find the softball team and rushed at once to the Hyatt.

Meanwhile, Star bureau chief Bill Norton, working late in the Johnson County bureau and listening to the police radio, heard calls for extra ambulances at the Hyatt. He immediately called assistant city editor Mike Zakoura, and the two of them began

Opposite: Front page of The Kansas City Star on July 19, 1981.

THE KANSAS CITY STAR.

★ *Sunday, July 19, 1981*

The Hyatt horror: 111 dead, 188 hurt and a city in shock

By Steve Woodward
and Robert J. Possek
staff writers

A gray sky rained tears Saturday on a city overcome with grief.

As bulldozers raked away tons of rubble that choked the once-glittering lobby of the Hyatt Regency hotel, funeral preparations began for the 111 persons killed when two massive aerial walkways plunged onto the crowded floor.

Saturday also marked the first painful day of recovery for the city and the 188 persons injured.

It was the nation's worst hotel disaster since a fire killed 119 in Atlanta in 1946,

and the worst loss of life since 274 persons died in the crash of a DC-10 airliner shortly after takeoff from Chicago's O'Hare International Airport in 1979.

The tragedy occurred shortly after 7 p.m. Friday when the 60-yard-long concrete and steel "skybridges" plunged onto a crowd attending a tea dance. Officials estimated the crowd at more than 1,500 persons, including dancers who stood on the aerial walkways and swayed to the music of the Steve Miller Band playing Duke Ellington's "Satin Doll."

As workers Saturday cleared mounds of bloody debris from the devastated lobby, there were these developments:

• Several investigations were

launched by the hotel's owner, Crown Center Redevelopment Corp., a subsidiary of Hallmark Cards Inc.; the hotel operator, Hyatt Hotels Corp.; the general contractor that built the hotel, Eldridge & Son Construction Co.; and the city of Kansas City.

• The year-old Hyatt Regency, the city's newest hotel and one of its three largest, was closed indefinitely.

• Speculation continued about the cause of the collapse, with eyewitnesses, building experts and hotel officials offering conflicting views.

• City Attorney Aaron Wilson refused to open city design and inspection records until officials review and catalog

them—despite an assurance by Mayor Richard Berkley Friday night that the records, normally open to the public, would be made available Saturday.

• The morgue at Truman Medical Center grew overloaded with bodies, forcing employees to stack bodies on the floor.

• Ambulance Services Inc., criticized in the past for slow response times, deployed seven vehicles to the hotel in less than 10 minutes, earning praise from city officials.

• Hyatt Hotels apparently told area hospital administrators the firm will pay the bills of persons injured at the hotel.

• Donors continued to stream into the Community Blood Center of Greater

Kansas City, 4040 Main.

• Members of the City Council met in a special informational session, and city, state and national leaders issued statements expressing sorrow over the tragedy.

Weary rescue workers, using huge cranes to lift the massive remnants of the two collapsed skywalks, worked through Friday night and into early Saturday morning to free the living and the dead.

An estimated 1,000 volunteers, firefighters, police officers and medics worked overnight to unravel the tangle of

See Horror, pg. 2HR, col. 1

Aftermath of a disaster . . . rescue workers and heavy equipment amid the rubble of the Hyatt Regency hotel lobby early Saturday.   (staff photo by Dan White © 1981 The Kansas City Star)

Critics contend failure of skywalk predictable

By Thomas G. Watts
staff writer

Echoes from the deadly avalanche of steel and concrete in the Hyatt Regency hotel Saturday included suggestions by some professional critics that the dangers might have been foreseeable.

"It was like pulling a staple through a piece of paper," was the way one local architect described how steel rods supporting the bridges above the hotel lobby tore away from their mooring.

One Kansas City structural engineer told The Star he found shortcomings in the engineering specifications after examining the debris in the hotel ballroom Saturday morning.

And an expert at the Kansas City Art Institute raised the issue of "harmonics

vibration," explaining that the swaying of people on the skywalks as they listened to the Tea Dance music could have touched off a similar movement in the bridges. That could have contributed to its failure, he said.

The architects, engineers and others who were involved in the construction of the hotel, however, were offering no theories about possible causes of the tragedy Saturday. They announced they were just launching investigations into possible structural flaws.

The local structural engineer—who refused to allow his name to be used because he feared he would be ostracized by his colleagues and his clients—said he believed suspension rods holding up the second- and fourth-story bridges had

See Critics, pg. 2HR, col. 6

Inside this section

• From ambulances to emergency rooms, they passed the supreme test. Page 2HR.

• Investigators are probing the cause of the skywalks' collapse. Page 3HR.

• A minute-by-minute account of the city's worst tragedy and its aftermath. Pages 4-5HR.

• A list of the dead and injured. Pages 4-5HR. (Obituaries of some of the victims are on Page 6R.)

• More color pictures, back page this section.

Vol. 101, No. 291
Main Edition. 20 sections, including STAR magazine.
50 cents.

Death at the Hyatt did not discriminate

By the Star's staff

When the walkways fell at the Hyatt Regency hotel Friday night, they made no distinction among those in the teeming lobby.

For many reasons—whether thirst or curiosity or fate—111 of those who found themselves on the west end of the hotel's lobby perished beneath that jagged tumble of concrete and steel.

But what the rescuers of their lives would be long and, inevitably, tragic. But here is a brief glimpse of some of them:

James S. Cottingham

James S. "Sam" Cottingham had a reputation for being a political kingpin in city government during his years as in-

dependence city counselor. But, as public, he downplayed his influence. He was known for his soft-deprecating wisecrack at council meetings and for a leavening running through less interesting discussions.

Cottingham resigned as city counselor in April of last year, following City Council elections in which the United Eastern Democrats' political faction won a complete majority.

Independence Mayor K. Lee Comer Jr. said Saturday, after learning of Cottingham's death, that many considered Cottingham to be among the best municipal attorneys in the state. He had served as regional vice president of the National Institute of Municipal Law Officers.

Cottingham was appointed an assistant

See Victims, pg. 7HR, col. 1

When it was all crumbling, we did what had to be done

By William D. Tammeus
A member of the editorial staff

This decent, civilized city, pummeled by a disaster of unthinkable proportions, honored its dead even as it sought to find them—honored them by its behavior.

The unspeakable horror of more than 100 crushed and dying bodies failed to unravel—and, in fact, revealed again—this fundamental goodness of Kansas City's people.

We were tested in a way that should happen to no one. And we did our part.

We did not dissolve into chaos. We rolled up our sleeves. We did what had to be done.

We helped each other even as we helped the injured. Injured people who had barely escaped death Friday night at the Hyatt Regency hotel immediately tried to pull others out of the wreckage. Hospitals, firemen, police, ambulances—all the necessary institutions of disaster—were there when we needed them, functioning exactly as we would have wanted them to.

"You had the feeling of real compassion about the people who were there helping," said Walt Bodine, the radio

talk show host who quickly gave up Friday dinner plans with friends to spend the entire night on the air keeping a stunned city up to date on the catastrophe's incredible magnitude.

Everywhere there was cooperation.

The people who watched these damnable hotel skywalks collapse near their heads quickly moved to rescue survivors. And soon they were helping hotel employees, police, firemen, paramedics, passers-by and reporters who, seen to record the carnage, helped to comfort and care for its victims.

Almost as soon as radio and TV stations put out a call for blood donors, the

Community Blood Center at 4040 Main was overwhelmed with volunteers. People wanting to give their blood to help save the bloodied victims formed a three-abreast line 50 yards long.

But there was much, much more. Nearly everyone who had anything to do with this disaster lost many has a story to tell today about some kind of heroism, and you will find some of these stories in today's paper. They will make you cry.

These point is that this tragedy brought out the best in us.

For people who know this city and its people, that is not s- surprising, too.

sometimes we put on a tough front. We say that we are from Missouri so you have to "show me," but the fact is that Kansas Citians are open and trusting people. When a brand new hotel is built, we trust that it will not fall down in a year and kill our friends and family. We are honest, trustworthy people, and expect nothing less in others.

And what we found.

There is no excuse for that happening in a virtually new building, said Mayor Richard L. Berkley. And, of course, he is right.

See Comment, pg. 2HR, col. 5

calling staff members to send to the hotel and the newspaper. Just before the three wives tracked us down at the Bigger Jigger, Zakoura reached us with the news. I dispatched several reporters to various city hospitals and sent the rest of the softball team to the newspaper.

I immediately drove to The Star and headed to the second floor newsroom, which the Star's staff shared with its rival sister paper, *The Kansas City Times.* The Times editors were busy trying to get organized for the Saturday morning editions, so I sent all Star staff members to the third floor features newsroom, which became The Star's headquarters for the next several hours. The Star, an afternoon and Sunday newspaper, didn't publish on Saturdays so it had 24 hours to prepare for Sunday's editions.

Just minutes before, about 1,500 people mostly from Kansas City were enjoying the regular Friday night tea dance at the hotel, owned by the Crown Center subsidiary of Hallmark, the highest regarded company in the city. Dozens of patrons were on the three 60-yard-long skywalks suspended over the lobby swaying to the music of the Steve Miller band playing Duke Ellington's "Satin Doll." Hundreds of others were dancing below or standing under the skywalks.

And suddenly, the fourth- and second-floor skywalks, constructed over one another, plunged onto the crowded floor, raining thousands of tons of concrete and steel that killed and maimed countless dozens. A day later when the wreckage was cleared, the toll was 113 dead and more than 200 injured, many severely. One of the injured died several weeks later, bringing the death toll to 114.

Zeeck, Levings and Alm arrived at the hotel minutes before the first police and fire responders showed up. Alm was drawn to the awesome wreckage in the lobby and recalls having a sense of being the only living person in the building. "There was an eerie silence," Alm says, "with only the sound of gushing water from a broken water main. I didn't venture much deeper into the hotel than the first 25 feet or so. I slowly walked around the wreckage of the skywalks, not knowing what had occurred."

And then it hit him like a sledgehammer. "I can still see the horrific images of human beings and parts of human beings crushed under the tons of concrete and steel."

Within minutes, police and fire responders were swarming into the lobby wreckage. At first they thought Alm was a victim. But when he identified himself as a reporter, they ordered him outside, where he started interviewing victims who had escaped the collapse.

Levings entered through a side entrance from the parking lot—the front entrance was blocked by mountains of glass shattered by the collapsing skywalks. He quickly found himself standing on the third-floor skywalk, which was set off to the side and had not collapsed.

"From there I had a great view of hell," Levings said. "The dust was still floating. I saw the rescuers crank up the concrete saws and add blue smoke to the haze. I watched as the Belger Co. crane moved in to poke through the glass. I noticed the clock from across the street and started noting the time of everything (this became a key component of a minute-by-minute chronology of the tragedy published in Sunday's Star)."

Eventually, police discovered Levings and asked him to leave. Outside, he ran into Zeeck, who determined they would be more useful back at The Star. They joined me on the third floor of The Star and we began planning for the Sunday newspaper. By then dozens of staff members had shown up at the paper as word of the tragedy spread around the city.

As a managing editor for less than three years, I was still struggling with how much of the job was managing and how much was editing. Every previous job I had was all editing or reporting. I loved editing and designing pages. But I knew that,

Dave Zeeck, city editor of
The Kansas City Star when
the Hyatt skywalks collapsed.

as managing editor, each time I became the hands-on editor, I blocked an opportunity for some other editor to make decisions and gain experience.

The Hyatt tragedy became an opportunity to pass the editing baton to Zeeck. So I offered some ideas but mainly served as an adviser. Zeeck consulted me on the coverage plan but all I did was affirm his approach. It was a big test for Zeeck, and he passed with flying colors, as I knew he would.

We divided the coverage into five major teams and made instant assignments to more than 100 editors, reporters and photographers.

Team One was headed by assistant city editor Rick Lyman and focused on stories of the victims, survivors and heroes on the scene and a step-by-step chronology of what had happened.

Levings headed Team Two, whose assignment was to track down the cause of the collapse, hunting for all city records, such as building inspections and blueprints, pertaining to the three-year-old hotel.

Team Three, led by assistant city editor Greg Edwards, was responsible for covering the emergency response.

Book editor Steve Paul headed Team Four, which focused on compiling obituaries of those killed and other Hyatt stories not covered by the first three teams.

Team Five consisted of me, Marty Petty, the assistant managing editor of photo and graphics, and Jim McTaggart, the photo editor, who oversaw the photo and design work for the next 24 hours.

We made dozens of decisions in the early hours following the tragedy but none more important than one born of past experience. A few years earlier, the roof of the city's Kemper Arena had collapsed. No one was in the building at the time so there were no deaths or injuries. But in covering the collapse, The Star never was able to pinpoint its cause because it lacked the expertise to interpret the design and building documents.

This time, we decided we needed help. We asked the Levings team to find a structural engineer willing to advise us.

Meanwhile, the Times was rushing toward deadline down on the second floor. The editor of both papers, Mike Davies, had arrived at The Times by 8 p.m. and helped oversee its coverage. Davies had tracked down The Star and Times' legendary publisher, Jim Hale, who was on his boat at the Lake of the Ozarks. He informed Hale of the collapse and warned that in the next few weeks the papers' cost in extra newsprint and overtime would be monumental. Hale had only one instruction for Davies: "Spend whatever it takes but get it right."

The Times was handicapped by several factors, including having only four hours to produce a newspaper (the first edition went to press at 11 p.m.). In addition, it was missing several staff members and two of its key editors, all enjoying a long weekend off. Managing editor Chris Waddle and city editor Paul Haskins were on a fishing trip to the Lake of the Ozarks and couldn't make the four-hour return trip in time to help lead the effort. Despite this, under the leadership of assistant managing editors Steve Shirk and Monroe Dodd, The Times acquitted itself well by producing five full pages of coverage by the final edition.

On the third floor, The Star teams, except for those assigned to all-night duty at the Hyatt, wound up their work about 1 a.m. Saturday with a memo from Zakoura outlining what everyone was to do starting at daybreak. Most of the editors were back on the job at 6 a.m., now working in the second-floor newsroom that had been vacated by The Times. By 9 a.m. the entire staff of about 175 was in the newsroom or out covering the story. Shortly after noon, 20 major stories were anticipated and deadlines for each were established. One of the most difficult to assemble was the compiling of the list of the dead and injured. Police reporter Greg Reeves had completed his work on stories involving the emergency response and joined reporter John Wylie's team, which was having difficulty getting a list of the victims and verifying the names.

At 7 p.m., just a couple of hours before the first edition deadline, the police had released the names of only 43 dead. Reeves spent the next 90 minutes contacting all his police sources to obtain a complete list. To get it, he went to the police command post at 28th and Main streets and helped them organize and type up the list in exchange for being the first person to obtain it. Armed with Reeves' list, reporter Bill Wilson and others on the victim team wrote brief biographies on most of those killed. Because of Reeves' efforts, The Star had a list of 111 dead four hours earlier than the police press officers at headquarters and in time for the first edition.

The Star's coverage was outstanding, filling a special 10-page section that wrapped around all the news sections, including the regular Page One and A section. An extra 30,000 copies were added to the regular press run of 417,000 and sold out within a few hours.

The staff was jubilant at its efforts and the resulting special section as it came off the press. Wylie summed up his colleagues feelings when he later wrote that "no one staff member deserves special recognition. This was a team effort, by far the best I've seen in the six-plus years I've been at this newspaper. Everyone pitched in to do whatever was needed at a given moment."

Features editor Stephanie Summers was impressed by "a pervasive mood of camaraderie and cooperation." Zeeck concurred. "Information was shared all over the room," he said. "Things went amazing well. Too bad more than 100 people had to die for us to work so well. That's when we began to feel guilty."

But much of the real work had not yet begun.

By midday Sunday, the Levings team had talked to several engineers and finally found one to agree to be an on-the-record consultant. All except one begged off for fear of being ostracized by the local architectural community. His name was Wayne Lischka, a structural engineer from Prairie Village, Kan.

In addition, reporter Tom Watts had identified another engineer who agreed to serve as an off-the-record consultant who would recheck all the Lischka findings but never be named in any story. Thus any Star story dealing with the Hyatt's structure had the independent approval of at least two engineers.

We put them to work immediately.

Lischka, wearing a Kansas City Star identification badge, accompanied Star photographer Talis Bergmanis on a city-sanctioned tour of the site Monday morning, with Lischka showing Bergmanis what pieces of the wreckage to photograph.

The city had agreed Sunday morning to allow the press to view the building's records but changed its mind later in the day. After hours of negotiation, the city agreed that first The Times and then The Star could have access for 30 minutes each on Monday to see the records but could not remove them.

By then, we had formed a mini-team of Watts, Alm and Lischka, reporting to Levings and Zeeck. Watts, the Jackson County courthouse reporter, was a conservative, cautious reporter and a fanatic for "getting it right." He was the perfect balance for Alm, equally dedicated to accuracy but aggressive and bold in his approach. The two of them and Lischka became nearly the perfect team.

Early Monday afternoon, Alm and Lischka were granted access at City Hall to design and architectural drawings, construction plans, specifications for the project and other Hyatt documents. They photographed and copied all the documents they could in their 30 minutes. But Alm had an advantage over everyone else who would get access to the documents. He was armed with a page number to copy, provided by Watts' silent partner, the anonymous engineer, who suspected a design flaw was a key factor in the collapse.

Alm and Lischka struck pay dirt.

Watts then took copies of the documents and the photographs to his engineer source for his inspection. He verified what he suspected and what Lischka already had determined: a major design change had been made, doubling the stress on the second- and fourth-floor skywalks.

The reporters, Lischka and editors Zeeck and Levings started putting the story together, working through the night until about 3 a.m. They were in the newsrooms when I arrived at 6 a.m. and began the final edit on their story.

And so on Tuesday afternoon, July 21, just four days after the Hyatt skywalks had collapsed, The Star led the paper with a blockbuster story under the bylines of Alm and Watts:

"A critical change in the original design of the Hyatt Regency hotel's skywalks doubled the stress on that part of the walks that later pulled apart during the collapse, The Star has found.

"City records—in combination with visual examination by two experts and photographic evidence—reveal that at some point a change was made that doubled the stress on three steel 'box beams' supporting the fourth floor skywalk.

"It was those beams that tore downward and away from their ceiling-anchored moorings, and both that walkway and a second story walkway hanging below plummeted to the hotel lobby."

The story also said that Lischka determined that the box beams under the top skywalk tore away from nuts that were on the lower ends of steel suspension rods that remained anchored in the ceiling. The story was accompanied by an artist's drawings of the original design and of the design that eventually was constructed.

The Alm-Watts-Lischka team wrote many more stories in the next several months adding more information on how the collapse occurred.

In January 1982, the U.S. Bureau of Standards released its report on the Hyatt collapse and cited The Star's stories for being 100 per cent accurate in pinpointing the cause. Eventually, the engineers who had signed off on the skywalk design change lost their licenses and the victims and families were awarded more that $140 million in judgments and settlements of civil lawsuits.

In April 1982, The Star and Times jointly were awarded the Pulitzer Prize in the general local reporting category for coverage of the Hyatt collapse. It was not without controversy. The Pulitzer jurors had recommended *The Miami Herald* and *The St. Petersburg Times* ahead of the Kansas City entry. But the Pulitzer board, in a somewhat unusual move, overruled the jurors and elevated the Hyatt coverage.

Thus the staffs of both The Star and The Times—about 320 journalists—could share in a Pulitzer Prize, proving that teamwork pays dividends.

How You Can Champion Teamwork: Learn to get your satisfaction through the success of others. Be prepared to make sacrifices for the team's overall good. Build up your teammates, not yourself. Honor your commitments and help to build trust. Help new team members when they join the group. Make sure each team has the necessary talent to be successful.

CHAPTER 6:

Be An Agent of Change

"If you have always done it that way,
it is probably wrong."

—INVENTOR CHARLES KETTERING

When Drew Gilpin Faust, the president of Harvard University, became chair of the Department of American Civilization at the University of Pennsylvania in 1980, she thought it was time to shift the focus. So she began pushing for change in an organization that was devoted to its past. Early on she encountered friction and a resistance to change.

What Dr. Faust experienced is all too common in organizations attempting to change.

When I was recruited by publisher and editor Mike Davies to be executive editor of *The Hartford Courant* in 1986, it was because Davies wanted to ramp up the pace of change at the paper. In many ways The Courant was a good paper but not improving fast enough to satisfy Davies. Within a month after my arrival and discussions with dozens of Courant journalists, it became clear that this was going to be a difficult task, mainly because most of the staff was reeling from huge change in the previous few years.

The Times Mirror Co. had purchased the independently owned Courant in 1979 and shortly thereafter appointed a Los

Angeles Times editor as the chief editor. He then replaced a handful of long-time Courant editors with Times editors, none of whom had much knowledge or a sense of Connecticut or New England. Worse yet, they didn't think they needed any.

The former Times editors quickly abandoned the 200-year-old mission of The Courant of being the bulletin board for Connecticut by covering news in nearly all the state's 169 towns. Their vision was of a Courant reporting mainly only the most important news of Connecticut, New England and the nation and leaving much of the local town news to smaller competitors.

But Connecticut's government structure was unusual. Each town had its own separate government, with individual school systems, police and fire departments, zoning boards and other government agencies. Unlike most other areas of the country, there was no county government incorporating several towns. Thus, covering local news meant covering each of the towns, a labor-intensive chore.

Furthermore, residents strongly identified with their towns. I remember being startled in my first meeting with company officials at the conglomerate United Technologies. They were much more interested in discussing The Courant's coverage of the towns in which they lived than in the coverage of the company.

Readers reacted swiftly and harshly to the new direction. They held demonstrations of protest, flooded the papers with angry telephone calls and letters and began canceling their subscriptions.

By 1983, Times Mirror was forced to make a change. It hired Davies, the editor of *The Kansas City Star and Times,* as both editor and publisher of The Courant. Davies moved quickly to change the mission again. He reinstituted much of the town news coverage and started zoning the news, eventually increasing the number of editions from two to seven. He also made it clear he wanted more emphasis on investigative and explanatory journalism within the region.

The new mission, with the new editions, required much more work so The Courant added about 50 journalists, which with the extra editions increased the complexity of the operation. Much of the staff, while generally supportive of the changes, was overwhelmed by them.

It was in to that culture that I arrived in March of 1986. I believed that more change was needed if we were to improve, but I thought the shell-shocked staff would revolt at any more change ordered from the top. Nevertheless, I believed that most of the staff wanted to improve the quality of the paper. I decided that if they became the agents of change the improvements would be their ideas and would be embraced better and longer than changes from on high.

So we announced the beginning of a series of staff critiques of the newspaper. Participation was voluntary. The process worked like this: a panel of five journalists would be assigned to critique all editions of the paper for two weeks on a particular subject, write a report with recommendations for improvement and hold a town meeting to discuss their findings. I promised to react instantly at the meeting to their recommendations.

The 10 topics we chose for the critique panels included writing lead paragraphs, overall writing, headline writing, photojournalism and coverage of town news. Dozens of staff members volunteered for each topic.

Davies and a few other senior editors were leery of this approach. They thought the critique panels would recommend only unrealistic and costly solutions to problems and abandon the daily coverage of news in the 69 towns, a mission about which many staff members complained constantly.

I believed that about 90 per cent of their suggestions would be the same ones most of us would recommend and we were taking very little risk in allowing them to lead the way. I also argued that we needed to select only their best recommendations, not all of them.

It turned out I was right.

The panels studied the paper, issued their reports and held town meetings at the nearby YMCA (The Courant's building was undergoing a major renovation). More than 300 of the 370 staff members attended most of the sessions. It was not difficult reacting instantly to their recommendations because we had their written reports several days before the town meetings.

At the session on overall writing, the panel recommended—perhaps demanded is more accurate—that the paper hire a writing coach. I was always a bit leery of writing coaches but still thought we needed one. Yet I believed any writing coach we hired would be seen as being forced on the staff and shunned by most. So when the writing panel urged the hiring of a writing coach, I responded at the town meeting that we would post the position at once.

We did, and a month later we promoted one of our senior writers, Bruce DeSilva, to writing coach. That would lead to more dramatic and transformational change in the next few years (more about that in Chapter 10).

The 10 critique panels finished their work in about 18 months. From the very first topic—on how to write better leads to stories—the changes in the paper began showing up. Within just a few months, the paper was changing in dozens of ways. The culture was electric—staff members saw that many of the changes they wanted were being instituted. The excitement was contagious. And it led in the next few years to several national journalism awards, including the newspaper's first Pulitzer, the 1992 Pulitzer Prize for Explanatory Journalism for a series about the flawed Hubble Telescope.

All institutions must continuously improve, change and adapt to new environments. Good leaders must show the way. One of the best methods is involving employees in leading the change.

CHAPTER 6: BE AN AGENT OF CHANGE

How You Can Be An Agent Of Change: Be ready to adapt quickly to organizational changes. Enlist all your employees in helping identify and institute change. Increase communications and constantly remind everyone of the overall goals. Alter the reward systems to match the change you are seeking.

Marty Petty
CEO
of Creative Loafing, Inc.

Leadership Sketch No. 3

Marty Petty joined Creative Loafing as chief executive officer in 2010. The company publishes weekly newspapers in several cities, including Washington, D.C., Chicago, Atlanta, Charlotte and Tampa.

For 27 years before that, she served in various newspaper executive positions. From 2000 to 2010 she was executive vice president and then publisher of The St. Petersburg Times. She worked for The Hartford Courant from 1983 to 2000, first as managing editor, then as deputy executive editor and associate publisher before moving to the business side where she held several positions, including senior vice president and general manager. She was promoted to publisher in 1997. Her newspaper career also includes editing positions at The Kansas City Star and Times, where she was a member of two Pulitzer Prize teams.

Marty earned a bachelor's degree in journalism in 1975 from the University of Missouri and a master's of science degree in management in 1989 from the Hartford Graduate Center.

She is president of the Florida Press Association Board and a former president and founder of the Society of Newspaper

Design. In 2005, Marty was named Distinguished Business Woman of the Year by the St. Petersburg Area Chamber of Commerce and Media Business Woman of the Year by the Tampa Bay Business Journal.

Marty's key leadership tips are:

• **Ride the trucks.** During a union organizing attempt, I spent six months riding the trucks with the circulation drivers and learned that almost all employee disgruntlement boils down to their desire for respect and for a clear understanding of expectations. Get out with your team, experience their challenges and hear their concerns.

• **Make more deposits than withdrawals.** Relationships between you and colleagues and employees are like a joint savings account. When you seek help from someone, you're making a withdrawal. When you volunteer to assist someone, you're making a deposit. Be sure to nurture workplace relationships and make more deposits than withdrawals.

• **Never use someone else's name to get something done.** Using "the boss said" to get something done indicates that you haven't developed a good enough relationship to influence the outcome. Strong relationships are the key to high-performing teams and organizations.

• **Keep commitments.** If you say you'll do it, then do it. People remember whom they can count on.

CHAPTER 7:

Excel as an Apostle of Hope

"If you must doubt something, doubt your limits."

—MANAGEMENT AND LEADERSHIP ADVISER PRICE PRITCHETT

Anyone who was a freshman in college in the 1950s and 1960s knows the story well. During the first week of orientation at an assembly hall, one of the deans tells the freshmen to look to their left and their right and declares, "One of the three of you will not graduate."

Such are the words of a disciple of doom.

An apostle of hope would have put it this way: "Look to your left and to your right. Our job is to make sure all three of you graduate."

Employees want leaders who are positive and hopeful. Not blindly optimistic Pollyannas, but truth-telling leaders who promote a can-do spirit.

One of the most remarkable projects of hope with which I was ever associated was Reading By 9, an inspiring five-year attempt to measurably increase the percentage of nine-year-olds in the Baltimore area able to read at, or above, grade level in the third grade.

It was born out of the experience of the wife of *The Sun's* editor, John Carroll. Lee Carroll was employed by the Baltimore

Curriculum Project, sponsored by the Abell Foundation, to develop curricula for the city's worst-performing schools. Each night Lee would come home and tell John how badly the city schools were doing. In 1997, only 11.2 percent of third graders in Baltimore city schools could read at grade level. Maryland students didn't fare all that much better—only one-third of 9-year-olds in the state could read at grade level. Even in the state's most prosperous county, Howard, barely more than 50 per cent of third-graders could read at grade level.

One Baltimore city school, City Springs, had no third graders reading at grade level, a phenomenon that occurred every year without any sense of alarm. The failure of these children was simply accepted. Carroll got increasingly interested in reporting on the problem and thought it was the answer to one of the big obstacles confronting journalists trying to cover education—namely the vast number of problems in the city schools. "I came to see the issue of reading by third grade as a vital sign—perhaps the most important vital sign—of a school system," Carroll says. "If you can't read, you can't learn anything, not math or anything else. Also, I learned, children who don't learn to read by third grade become behavior problems and eventually end up in the criminal justice system."

At about the same time, Mark Willes, the new CEO of the Times Mirror Co., owner of *The Sun,* had declared the core purpose of Times Mirror was "to improve the performance of society by seeking truth and sharing understanding." He invited all the newspaper editors in the company to Los Angeles to present their ideas aimed at improving society.

Carroll presented his Reading by 9 idea and its core mission: to focus an unrelenting spotlight on a single question—are the schools teaching their children to read by third grade? Willes loved it, as did Sun publisher Mary Junck, who had already thrown vast resources at the project by the time I replaced her in September 1997 (Mary was promoted to president of Time Mirror's Eastern newspapers).

Reading By 9 wasn't just a journalism project. *The Sun* enlisted more than 200 employee volunteers to teach reading each week in several city schools. Student attendance and morale increased on the days tutors were to appear—the program could have been named Hope By 9. It not only inspired students but also Sun employees.

To help defray expenses of adding about five pages of coverage each week, the Marketing and Advertising Departments recruited corporate sponsors who paid as much as $200,000 a year to join the effort. Leading the way were Legg Mason, Bell Atlantic, the Baltimore Gas & Electric Co, First National Bank of Maryland and the University of Maryland School of Medicine. All of them provided volunteers to teach reading in the schools.

A four-day series in *The Sun* kicked off the project on Nov. 2, 1997. It explored why many children weren't learning to read properly, detailed research supporting reading instruction that began with teaching the sounds that make up words, pointed out that methods of reading instruction often varied widely within in the same school district and revealed that most teacher-training colleges didn't prepare their graduates to teach beginning reading. The series wound up with a list of the reading scores for three years in more than 360 elementary schools in central Maryland. Each time the state conducted another test, The Sun listed all the scores with the previous years.

City Springs Elementary School became a special case, luring several corporate sponsors and hundreds of reading volunteers and prompting frequent progress reports in *The Sun*. Not surprisingly, the school's performance improved dramatically.

For five years, *The Sun* produced parent and child pages each week for kids to read as well as other weekly features. In addition, the newspaper wrote more than 300 major stories about every facet of the reading problem, including a report from the Moscow bureau's Kathy Lally that explained an ongoing phonics debate in Russia. Many of the stories focused on successes in the classroom and on the schools and principals who were making the most progress.

The Sun served as a convener for educators, literacy organizations, the business community, parents and other concerned groups to collaborate on efforts to improve reading. Its media partnerships with WBAL-TV and Radio One promoted reading messages every day and it sponsored book give-aways, targeting low-income areas.

The newspaper also sponsored annual awards for the best reading teachers and librarians and a Champions Readers Program. Students who got "A's" in reading won a special night at the National Aquarium and a day at the Maryland Science Center.

Meanwhile, the Maryland Department of Education, always seeking reform under its innovative superintendent, Nancy Grasmick, instituted major public policy changes, including significantly increasing requirements for teacher certification. School districts across Maryland declared reading the No. 1 priority. The Baltimore city schools implemented a new reading program for grades 1-3.

Grasmick frequently said in public meetings that these public policy reforms could not have been instituted without the relentless coverage of the issue by *The Sun*.

The end result was impressive. In 2002, five years after the beginning of Reading By 9, Maryland third graders reading at or above grade level had increased to 51 per cent, 18 percentage points better than in 1997. In the Baltimore city schools, the number increased from 11.2 percent in 1997 to 32 per cent in 2002.

Hopeful leaders get positive results. Negative ones don't keep their jobs for long.

How You Can Be An Apostle Of Hope: Good golfers, when preparing for the next shot with water hazards and sand traps lurking, focus on where they want to hit the ball, not where they don't want to hit it. The same is true in the workplace. Focus on the positives and on what you want to achieve, not on the hazards that stand in your way. Be a cheerleader and help people gain confidence.

CHAPTER 8:

Be A Slave To Integrity

---

*"If leaders are careless about telling the truth
and respecting moral codes, who can believe them
on other issues?"*

—EDUCATOR JAMES L. HAYES

Leaders need several traits to succeed but few are more important than integrity and its first cousin, character.

Robert Mazzuca, chief executive of the Boy Scouts of America, is a huge believer in the Scout Law: Be trustworthy, loyal, helpful, friendly, courteous, kind, obedient, cheerful, thrifty, brave, clean and reverent. "Charisma and other personality traits may determine how far up the ladder you go, but the 12 points of the Scout Law define your character," Mazzuca says. "If you don't have integrity, you're not a good leader no matter how charismatic."

When speaking to a leadership forum in Hartford in the 1990s, Gen. Norman Schwarzkopf defined leadership as competency and character, adding that if he could choose only one trait, it would be character.

Among my favorite examples of integrity and character in the newspaper business was that displayed by Jim Hale, publisher of *The Kansas City Star and Times* when the Hyatt Regency Crown Center Hotel skywalks collapsed on July 17, 1981. The tragedy killed 114 and injured more than 200 (details of the coverage are in Chapter 5). As the newspapers reported on the disaster for the next several months (The Star alone published more than 350 stories), the pressure mounted on Hale from community leaders to stop the coverage.

Hale, publisher of the papers in the 1970s and 1980s, had risen over the years from various news and business-side jobs in several small newspapers to publisher of *The Star-Telegram* in Fort Worth, Tex. He was promoted to publisher of the Kansas City papers when they were purchased in 1977 by Capital Cities, Inc.

Integrity was not necessarily a constant companion of Hale, a great businessman who was at times brilliant, often generous, always funny but occasionally cruel and less than truthful. But integrity and character visited him during the Hyatt Regency ordeal.

The owner of the Hyatt was a subsidiary of Hallmark, an outstanding company and the most popular one in Kansas City. Within a few weeks many city business leaders came to believe that the constant coverage was giving Kansas City a black eye. Some of them paraded to New York City to meet with Tom Murphy and Dan Burke, the CEO and president, respectively, of Capital Cities, Inc. They demanded that the coverage stop and that Hale and editor Mike Davies be removed. Murphy and Burke listened politely but told them that Capital Cities followed a policy of leaving all coverage decisions to the local publishers and editors. They added that their only recourse would be to convince Hale.

Hale had other visitors. Representatives of the Pritzker family in Chicago, long-time owners and managers of Hyatt Regency Hotels, met with him and expressed their displeasure over a Times story involving them. They pointed out that there could be consequences for Capital Cities broadcast stations when it came time to renew their government licenses.

But the views of many Kansas City readers were just the opposite. They were best summed up by Janet Nolte in a letter to the editors of The Star:

"People I love were killed and hurt in the disaster and I want to know why...I was sure there would be an honest effort made. This feeling was reinforced when I read the statement of grief from Donald Hall...I was a little irritated when the Kansas City Star hired its own investigator just as the architects, Crown Center, Hyatt and everyone else hired their own.

"Today, I fear only the Star's investigator is free to investigate. Self-preservation would seem to have overcome human love and concern. The Hyatt appears terrified someone will find out anything. The Mayor's hands are tied, though he desperately keeps trying. Donald Hall is not available and the lawyers of the area don't really care what caused the disaster because they have more than enough evidence to win their cases. The City Council is scared to death it is the fault of their inspectors....

"That leaves The Star. Please find out for us what happened so we can make sure it will never happen again."

The Star did just that, as Jim Hale, in one of his great shining moments, didn't flinch as he deflected the critics and constantly reminded us to "get it right."

It's difficult not to conclude that integrity and character in the face of adversity are among the most important leadership traits.

How You Can Be A Slave To Integrity: Integrity means not cheating or cutting corners. It means living up to your word and not promising things you can't deliver. Most of all, it means doing the right thing even if it's painful.

Mike Mulvain
owner and operator of
Mulvain Woodworks in Durand, Ill.

Leadership Sketch No. 4

Mike Mulvain graduated from Durand High School in 1960 and attended Whitewater State College in Wisconsin until he started working in 1962 for the Weyerhaeuser Company in Rockford, Ill.

He held various positions in the production, accounting and scheduling departments before being promoted to a supervisor's position. He later became a manager and shift superintendent. He spent the next several years as operations manager for the production department, overseeing nine supervisors and 150 employees and representing the company in union negotiations. During this time, he was an instructor in supervisor and leadership training.

Mike retired from Weyerhaeuser in 1990 and started his own business. He bought a Woodmizer sawmill and began learning about and producing wood products. His wife, a nurse, joined him in the venture in 1995 and the company of eight employees has become very successful in manufacturing and selling such wood products as custom moldings, hardwood floors and custom cabinets and services in Northern Illinois and Southern Wisconsin.

Mike's key leadership tips are:

- **Be a model of integrity.** You must be honest with your customers and your employees.
- **Delegate responsibility.** Empower your employees to fulfill their responsibilities and hold them accountable. Be generous with praise.
- **Develop other leaders.** You can't succeed as a "go-it-alone" manager. You must take people along with you on the journey of personal growth.
- **Communicate clearly and listen.**
- **Get the right people in the right jobs.**
- **Know your employees on a personal level.** That way you can support and encourage them, especially when they are facing difficult times in the lives.

CHAPTER 9:

Communicate, Communicate, Communicate,

"Communication is the real work of leadership."

—NITIN NOHRIA, DEAN OF THE HARVARD BUSINESS SCHOOL

When we created the Leadership Model at *The Hartford Courant* in 1995 (details in Chapter 1), it was obvious that the 90 managers assigned to lead the company and make the key decisions needed the latest and best information available. So we released to them operational reports that included much information that previously had been available to only 15 top managers. Some of them argued that the previously confidential information would now be leaked to competitors and eventually be published by them. In six years under the Leadership Model, that never happened—all the managers honored the trust bestowed upon them.

In addition, each of the eight leadership committees issued reports to the 90 managers on the status of its deliberations. Within a few months, the managers, who often previously felt they were in the dark, complained about having too much information to digest.

But it's never too much, according to Susan Docherty, leader of the U.S. sales, service and marketing team at General Motors.

"Whether you have a really small team or a really big team," she told *The New York Times,* "communications needs to be at the forefront. It needs to be simple. It needs to be consistent. And even when you're tired of what the message is, you need to do it again and again, because everybody comes to the table with a different perspective and a different experience. The same words mean different things to different people."

Many managers overestimate their ability to communicate. A survey of 1,100 front-line managers conducted by the consulting firm Development Dimensions International Inc. found that 50 per cent of them thought communications was a strength and less than 5 per cent thought they needed to improve. Any employee of nearly any company can tell you that few supervisors excel at communications.

Most of all, the communications need to be candid, sensitive to the listeners but candid nevertheless. If not, the chances of mimicking the Abilene Paradox increase. The Abilene Paradox, originated by Dr. Jerry B. Harvey, professor emeritus of management science at George Washington University, offers this vital lesson in communicating:

> The July afternoon in Coleman, Texas, (population 5,607) was particularly hot—104 degrees as measured by the Walgreen's Rexall Ex-Lax temperature gauge. In addition, the wind was blowing fine-grained West Texas topsoil through the house. But the afternoon was still tolerable—even potentially enjoyable. There was a fan going on the back porch; there was entertainment. Dominoes. Perfect for the conditions. The game required little more physical exertion than an occasional mumbled comment, "Shuffle 'em," and an unhurried movement of the arm to place the spots in the appropriate perspective on the table. All in all, it had the makings of an agreeable Sunday afternoon in Coleman—

that is, it did until my father-in-law suddenly said, "Let's get in the car and go to Abilene and have dinner at the cafeteria."

I thought, "What, go to Abilene? Fifty-three miles? In this dust storm and heat? And in an unaircondi-tioned 1958 Buick?"

But my wife chimed in with, "Sounds like a great idea. I'd like to go. How about you, Jerry?" Since my own preferences were obviously out of step with the rest, I replied, "Sounds good to me," and added, "I just hope your mother wants to go."

"Of course I want to go," said my mother-in-law. "I haven't been to Abilene in a long time."

So into the car and off to Abilene we went. My pre-dictions were fulfilled. The heat was brutal. We were coated with a fine layer of dust that was cemented with perspiration by the time we arrived. The food at the cafeteria provided first-rate testimonial material for ant-acid commercials.

Some four hours and 106 miles later we returned to Coleman, hot and exhausted. We sat in front of the fan for a long time in silence. Then, both to be sociable and to break the silence, I said, "It was a great trip, wasn't it?"

No one spoke.

Finally, my mother-in-law said, with some irritation, "Well, to tell the truth, I really didn't enjoy it much and would rather have stayed here. I just went along because the three of you were so enthusiastic about going. I wouldn't have gone if you all hadn't pressured me into it."

I couldn't believe it. "What do you mean, 'you all'?" I said. "Don't put me in the 'you all' group. I was delighted to be doing what we were doing. I didn't want to go. I only went to satisfy the rest of you. You're the culprits."

BLOOD ON THE OUT-BASKET

My wife look shocked. "Don't call me a culprit. You and Daddy and Mama were the ones who wanted to go. I just went along to be sociable and to keep you happy. I would have had to be crazy to want to go out in heat like that."

Her father entered the conversation abruptly. "Hell!" he said.

He proceeded to expand on what was already absolutely clear. "Listen, I never wanted to go to Abilene. I just thought you might be bored. You visit so seldom I wanted to be sure you enjoyed it. I would have preferred to play another game of Dominoes and eat the leftovers in the icebox."

After the outburst of recrimination, we all sat back in silence. Here we were, four reasonable, sensible people who, of our own volition, had just taken a 106-mile trip across a godforsaken desert in a furnace-like temperature through a cloud-like dust storm to eat unpalatable food at a hole-in-the-wall cafeteria in Abilene, when none of us had really wanted to go. In fact, to be more accurate, we'd done just the opposite of what we wanted to do. The whole situation simply didn't make sense.

One of the lessons of the Abilene Paradox is simple: Say what you mean and mean what you say.

How You Can Communicate, Communicate, Communicate: Share as much information as possible with as many people as possible. In this age of technology, do as much face-to-face communication as possible. Relying on email and written communications will only increase the chances that your message may be misinterpreted. And remember, you can't overcommunicate.

CHAPTER 10:

Teach and Coach

"When your time comes to pass on someday,
the only things you can keep are what you gave away."

—HARVEY PENICK, LEGENDARY FORMER GOLF TEACHER

AT THE AUSTIN COUNTRY CLUB

When Chief Executive magazine and Hay Group released the 2009 rankings of companies that are best at developing future leaders, 3M jumped to first place from 15th in 2008. CEO George Buckley, in an interview with *USA Today,* explained why teaching and coaching are so vital.

"Years ago when I worked at Brunswick (in a difficult economy), I was asked, should we be spending money on training? What if these people leave the company? My answer was, what if we don't and they stay?"

Buckley believes certain traits can't be taught. "There are things you are born with," he says. "You can't develop intelligence or morals by law...but there are things we can develop. Strategic thinking, for example. There is a difference between a leader and a manager. A leader is as much about inspiration as anything else. A manager is more about process. We try to mix both into our development. In the end, maybe you can't plant leadership in a person, but you certainly can enhance it in a person."

When asked why not save money on leadership development and recruit top talent from others, he replied: "I'd sooner own a fish farm that be reliant on catching a few fish."

At *The Hartford Courant* in 1988, we were trying to establish a fish farm when we named Bruce DeSilva writing coach following one of the many changes recommended by the staff in a series of critiques of the newspaper (details in Chapter 6). DeSilva's assignment was to assist writers without impeding their editors.

We started with a lofty goal: to transform The Courant into one of the best written newspapers in the country. That was different from most newspapers with writing-coach programs. Their idea was to work with a few writers and help them get better, making the paper slowly more readable. And many programs worked with writers who needed the most help.

We reversed the approach of giving the most attention to the weakest performers. Instead, DeSilva worked with the very best writers and the young writers with the most potential. His success was due in part by selling powerful ideas and beating back long-standing blockades to innovation.

His first attack was aimed at the myth of the newspaper. Every newspaper is built on a series of myths, including such things as "the public's right to know" and "freedom of the press." But they also include a lot of ideas specific to each newspaper, usually unspoken but vital in defining what kind of newspaper is being produced and reinforced daily by what appears on Page One.

The myth of the paper is the main reason *The New York Times* is different from *The New York Post.* It isn't just a matter of talent and resources. If the Times hired a Post copy editor, he would be the same person with the same skills. But he would suddenly start editing and writing headlines differently. For one thing, he would stop writing great headlines such as "Headless Body in Topless Bar" and instead write "Homicide

Suspected in Brooklyn Slaying." He would do this because he would be taught, "at The Times, (substitute any newspaper's name), this is the way we do things."

DeSilva attacked the myth by holding meetings with staff members. He presented them with examples of great writing from such papers as *The St. Petersburg Times* and *The Providence Journal* using particular story forms rarely used in The Courant, including the narrative style, *The Wall Street Journal* block organization, magazine-style profiles and first-person stories.

Bruce DeSilva, writing coach of The Hartford Courant.

Senior editors as well as writers attended the meetings and most loved the examples. But many pointed out that "we can't do that here." DeSilva asked "Why not?" "Because they won't let us," was the answer. So DeSilva went around the room and asked the editors whether they would want such a story in The Courant. The answer was always yes.

"Then it was your turn," DeSilva recalls, referring to me "You said, 'If we're so damned stupid that we wouldn't put this sucker on Page One, we all should have our asses fired.' I swear that is an exact quote. I remember it vividly. That was a huge moment. From then on, everyone had permission to do things differently. I don't think I ever heard 'they won't let us' again."

DeSilva then attacked The Courant's snake rules. Most newspapers have their snake rules—unbending commands that have existed so long that few staff members remember why they were ordained.

Snake rules got their name from Don Fry, a renowned writing coach who encountered them while conducting a workshop at a Midwestern newspaper. Fry was attending the editors' daily news conference where all the top stories were discussed. The editors agreed a story about snakes would be published the next day on the Metro section front. But the metro editor stressed that the photo of the snakes must be published inside the section, not with the story on the Metro front page. All the editors nodded in agreement.

Fry interceded. Why, he asked, would you not publish the photo of the snakes with the story on the Metro front? Because, he was told, photos of snakes on section fronts are banned here. Why? asked Fry. No one knew for certain.

Fry decided to try to find out why. Within hours, he got the rest of the story from a couple of veterans on the paper's copy desk. Their tale seemed absurd. Some 30 years ago the paper had published a photo of snakes on the front page. The wife of the publisher called the editor and complained vigorously. He reacted by ordering that henceforth photos of snakes would never be published on Page One or section front pages. The rule survived despite the death years ago of the publisher's wife and comings and goings of new publishers and editors.

Even more absurb, DeSilva encountered the same snake rule years later while teaching at a workshop at a newspaper owned by the same company. It had crossed state lines and multiplied.

The Courant, like most newspapers, had dozens of snake rules, such as never write in the first person or never begin a story with a quote. Some were formalized in a stylebook. Others were just generally understood. Some made sense but many others didn't. All were ruthlessly enforced by the copy desk. More got added every year but none ever got eliminated. The result was that the playing field for writers and editors kept getting smaller and the paper kept getting duller.

So DeSilva attacked. Every time someone said "we don't do that here" or "we always do it this way," he asked why. Sometimes the answers made sense, but a lot of times they didn't. And when the reasons seemed stupid, the dumb rules started dying like weeds sprayed with herbicide. By challenging the snake rules, DeSilva and other editors gave writers more options for telling their stories effectively.

Finally, DeSilva and other editors began creating a safe house—they preached that trying new approaches to stories was NOT taking a risk. Their message was that The Courant was a newspaper where it was safe to try new things and there was no penalty for failure.

The message wasn't immediately successful. Newsrooms are cover-your-ass places. Most journalists fear innovation and creativity. Experience has taught them that mediocrity never gets them in trouble. But within a few short months, when several writers had already produced outstanding stories using new story forms, most writers and editors began believing that it really was safe to try a new approach.

It helped that DeSilva's first effort was a big success. He picked seven talented writers, including Ed Mahony, Lynne Tuohy and Jack Ewing, to attend his first workshop on narrative storytelling, a form used only in The Courant's *Northeast* magazine. The group met for an hour a week for six weeks and together produced a story, with each sharing in the reporting and Mahony doing the writing, of a day in the life of the Hartford criminal courthouse. It was riveting and created much excitement in the newsroom.

DeSilva's narrative writing class became an instant hit. Staff members who signed up had to promise perfect attendance. DeSilva recruited a few of the best writers on the staff to help him teach the course, which was restricted to eight students. He also recruited renowned journalists as instructors. More than 50 staff members signed up after the first session and the waiting list eventually grew to more than a year.

It was the same pattern for other courses. Classes on storytelling and tight writing filled up immediately and had long waiting lists. An eight-week workshop designed for origination editors on how to edit The Courant had a year-and-a-half waiting list.

It wasn't long before dozens of terrific stories began appearing on The Courant's front pages. Kathy Megan wrote a compelling series about a heart transplant patient, Mary Otto profiled a group of heroin users living in a nice Hartford neighborhood that stunned readers, Mahony wrote an entertaining narrative serial about the adventures of an FBI undercover agent and Mark Pazniokas wrote a riveting narrative detailing the conspiracy of some Democratic legislators on how they plotted to overthrow the Speaker of the House.

The writing in The Courant was now catching up with the outstanding photojournalism that had been the paper's signature since the mid-1980s.

For the next few years, DeSilva continued teaching his workshops and doing a lot of one-on-one coaching, working with not just a writer but also with his editor. This was vital because it prevented the editor from feeling bypassed.

Throughout the process we were very clear about the kind of work we wanted, not by criticizing what we didn't like but by praising what we did like.

"And we made that praise very specific," DeSilva says. "No vague attaboys. You were particularly good at coming out of your office, plopping down on a writer's desk and telling him exactly what you liked about his story in the previous day's paper. You made a show of it. That way everybody within earshot knew what you liked and why. And everybody wanted to be the next person to get that kind of attention."

By the third year, DeSilva spread the power of coaching by teaching a lot of editors to be coaches. We developed one of the first programs anywhere for this kind of editor training. Within a year or so, many editors were coaching the entire process instead of just giving out assignments and waiting to edit the writer's final draft. They were editing people, not just copy.

At the same time, DeSilva established a formal mentoring program, one of the most successful writer-on-writer and editor-on-editor mentoring programs at a newspaper. It worked well for at least three reasons: we made it clear to everyone involved that the senior editors valued it, we paid close attention to make sure each pairing was working, and the mentors discovered the joy of teaching and realized the newspaper valued what they were doing. All of this activity helped staff members realize that they didn't have to change newspapers or even their jobs to have the opportunity to improve at their craft.

Not everything worked.

Some writers were hard to coach because they loved reporting but hated to write. Some editors were too willing to let DeSilva edit the entire story. And a few editors and writers, including a handful of the most talented people on the staff, interpreted everything DeSilva did as an effort not to improve the paper but to boost his career at everyone else's expense. They thought he was a glory hound and interpreted his praise of a story as an attempt to take credit for it. And they never really did embrace the program.

But most staff members did and helped us reach our goal. For at least eight years, The Courant was one the best written newspapers in America. It had become an exciting place to work and was easily one of the top 20 papers in the country.

But all of that started changing in 1996 and 1997, when DeSilva left the paper to become news/features editor of The Associated Press, directing its elite team of national writers, and eventually became its writing coach, and I left to become

publisher of *The Sun.* Assistant managing editor Bobbie Ross-
ner replaced DeSilva but her approach was much more limited.
The program began shrinking even more after Tribune Co.
acquired The Courant in 2000 and eventually died under the
Tribune's unenlightened leadership.

Nevertheless, coaching and teaching are among the most important responsibilities of leaders.

How You Can Teach And Coach: Correcting people's work on
deadline fixes the work but not the problem. Most people learn
very little under the pressure of deadline. Offering instruction in a
calmer, more private moment off-deadline is much more effective.
One of the best ways to teach is to simply ask questions. Employees most often will have the answers and the lessons will stick with
them. Meet informally at least once a month to discuss their work
and provide feedback. Surround any negative comments with a
heavy dose of positive.

John S. Carroll
former editor
The Los Angeles Times

Leadership Sketch No. X

John S. Carroll has been editor of three newspapers: The Los Angeles Times (2000-2005), The Sun in Baltimore (1991-2000) and The Lexington Herald-Leader (1979-1991). In 2006 he served as Knight Visiting Lecturer at the Kennedy School of Government, Harvard University.

He first became a reporter for The Providence Journal-Bulletin (1963-1964). At The Sun in his first tour of duty (1966-1972), he was posted to Vietnam, the Middle East and Washington. In the 1970s, he was metropolitan editor of The Philadelphia Inquirer. He has received several individual awards. As the editor in Lexington and Baltimore, his papers won four Pulitzer Prizes and in his five years as The Los Angeles Times editor 13 Pulitzer Prizes.

Carroll is a 1963 graduate of Haverford College and served from 1964 to 1966 in the Army. He was a Nieman Fellow at Harvard University in 1971-72 and had a similar fellowship at Oxford University in 1988. He served on the Pulitzer Prize Board from 1994 to 2003 and was its chairman in 2002. He is a fellow of the American Academy of Arts and Sciences and is the 2011 recipient of the William Allen White Award.

Carroll's key leadership tips are:

- **Don't try to impress people with what you know.** Instead, learn by listening to what they know.
- **Be a human being first and a manager second.**
- **The only personality that can lead to success is the one you've already got.**
- **Don't let meetings hold you hostage.** Make plenty of time every day for your own initiatives.
- **Talk freely with employees at all levels.** The chain of command only matters in making assignments. Don't let it stifle free speech.
- **Respect and celebrate your employees' skills.**

CHAPTER 11:
Listen, Really Listen

"My girlfriend says I never listen to her.
I think that's what she said."

—COMEDIAN DRAKE SATHER

William Mitchell, who in the 1970s worked for the Raychem company in Menlo Park, Calif., became bitten by the CEO bug. He knew his chances were slim at Raychem because the CEO was a young man.

But he was approached by the Nashua Corp., a manufacturing company in New Hampshire, whose CEO was ready to retire. He met some board members, who told him they wanted a more entrepreneurial direction, and he convinced them he was their man.

"I felt I was an irresistible force and I could do anything," he says. But he wound up failing. The reasons were many, but Mitchell cites these as among the most important ones: "I didn't listen well. I didn't do a good job of learning the business and I didn't build consensus. I went in thinking I knew all the answers." Fortunately, he learned his lessons well and is now CEO of Arrow Electronics.

Another CEO, Randy Bernard of the Indy Racing League, knows better. Bernard, who is new to Indy-style car racing, thinks "listening is the most important thing I can do. I want to listen to everyone. Not only the best driver in the world but also the 24th best driver. The No. 1 team owner and the smallest team owner. It is my job to make sure I can understand all their concerns, while at the same time do what is right."

Over the years hundreds of employees have come to me to discuss problems, professional and personal. I found that just by listening and asking a few questions the employees themselves came up with the answer 90 per cent of the time.

Gary McCullough, president and CEO of Career Education Corp., tells a story about the power of listening and small gestures when he was a platoon leader in the Army at Ft. Bragg, N.C.

"It had been raining for a week. The commanding general came by one of our exercises and asked one of the vehicle drivers what he thought of it. 'Sir, it stinks,' the private said. 'Why?' asked the general. "Because this is terrible weather to be doing infantry operations,' replied the private. 'What can I do to make it better for you?' asked the general. 'I sure could use a Snickers bar,' the private said.

"A couple of days later a box with 38 Snickers bars showed up for the private, with a note from the general saying 'I can't doing anything about the weather but I hope this makes your day a bit brighter. Please share these with your 37 platoon buddies.' And on that day, we would have followed that general anywhere."

All because he listened.

How You Can Listen, Really Listen: Pay attention when someone is speaking to you. Don't prepare what you'll say while they're talking. Look people in the eye. Before responding, repeat the message you think you've just heard to avoid misunderstandings. Remember that many people are not expecting answers; they just want someone to listen.

CHAPTER 12:
Embrace Innovation

*"In my business, if you stop being creative
and innovative, you're finished."*

—JEFFREY KATZENBERG, CEO OF DREAMWORKS ANIMATION SKG

Innovation is the lifeblood of most businesses, including news-papers. *The Hartford Courant's* Sunday magazine, *Northeast,* under the leadership of editor Lary Bloom, excelled at being cre-ative. And one of its most innovative projects was Art For All.

The project was associate editor Jan Winburn's idea but it sprung from a notion Bloom had years earlier. The Courant decided in 1981 to create a new Sunday magazine and hired as its first editor Bloom, then editor of *The Miami Herald's* award-winning Sunday magazine, *Tropic.* He was an outstanding edi-tor with a bundle of brainstorms. It was if he and his staff were on FM and the rest of the newsroom was on AM. Over time Bloom began noticing that many notable people—such as Paul Newman, Philip Roth, Calvin Klein and world-class academics, scientists and artists—had some Connecticut connection. As the years passed, Bloom would add names to his list on the wall as they surfaced in news accounts.

As 1986 approached—the state's 350th anniversary—the *Northeast* editors wanted to celebrate the state's history with a special issue. They decided on a creative approach they called

the Connecticut Celebrity Register—short profiles in one issue of 350 people who had made a difference in Connecticut.
The editors had one unbendable rule: all the subjects had to
be alive. And they decided to ask each of them to comment on
why they lived in Connecticut—a monumental logistical task in
itself.

The magazine's page capacity was 144, so Bloom negotiated with the advertising department for enough space for the
profiles. The ad department kept 71 pages (all sold out quickly
because it was a great advertising opportunity) and the news
department kept 73 pages for the profiles.

"It turned out to be the most complicated and demanding
task any of us had undertaken," Bloom says. "Just finding and
selecting the final 350 was arduous, as there were literally thousands of qualified candidates. How did the creator of McCall's
Sewing Patterns stack up against someone who had important
roles in eight movies? Those were the kinds of discussions we
had. But it was a time of great excitement, and we benefited
greatly from the enthusiasm of top management.

"When the issue finally appeared on May 18, 1986, there was
a great response. Even today I get requests for copies from a va-
riety of sources."

However, two days before publication of the special issue,
one of those profiled, author Teddy White, died. Within a couple of weeks, others including Big Band leader Benny Goodman
and actor Sterling Hayden died. That's when Winburn came up
with her idea. She, like Bloom, was a genius at helping writers
shape and improve their stories, so much so that writers in all
departments of the paper lined up in the hopes of getting their
turn to work with her. Winburn noted that the celebrities could
live anywhere they wanted but they chose Connecticut because
it was a sanctuary—much of their work appeared elsewhere
around the world. She wanted to enlist some of the state's

senior artists to do commissioned work for the people of Connecticut before it was too late.

But Winburn and Bloom faced a huge financial challenge: how to fund the project. After all, many of the artists they hoped to recruit earned huge sums for their work—hundreds of thousands of, and sometimes a million, dollars. The editors decided on an unprecedented kind of partnership—public art financed by private corporations, requiring a team of four: the corporation, the artist, the public place to display the work and *The Hartford Courant.*

The Courant's top management—editor and publisher Mike Davies, general manager Ray Jansen and me as executive editor—loved the idea and invited all the leading Hartford corporations to a breakfast at The Hartford Club to hear the idea.

So at 8 a.m. on Sept. 8, 1986, the captains of Hartford industry sat around the table in Room 22. They included Jim Lynn from The Aetna, James McNally from Connecticut Bank and Trust, Dick Ayers from Stanley Works, Joel Alvord from Connecticut National Bank, Wilson Wilde from Hartford Steam Boiler, Ray D'Argenio from United Technologies and Elliot Gerson from the Travelers.

They listened intently as Winburn and Bloom pitched their idea. They put on a slide show starring many of the artists included in their Connecticut Celebrity Register. They were proposing something we had never seen in the newspaper business, a kind of civic journalism in which all the parties—the newspaper, the corporations, the artists and the public—would benefit. Each company would fund its project and would be matched with a senior artist in the state who would create a unique work of art that would be displayed in a public place—a park, a hospital, a school, an airport—for all to see. Each artist would be profiled in Northeast magazine, with the logo of the company commissioning the work appearing alongside. Each company would get a plaque and be saluted at a recognition dinner. Once the project was completed, the artists' works would be photographed and published in *Northeast's* sixth anniversary edition.

But how much would the art cost? That was the unspoken question hovering over the presentation by Winburn and Bloom until at last Lynn raised his hand and asked it. Winburn and Bloom talked around it, saying it was hard to know, depending on whether it was a painting or a large sculpture requiring foundry work. But they finally spit it out: a minimum of $15,000, perhaps more.

"Oh, I thought we were talking about real money here," replied a relieved Lynn. "It can cost that much to hire a speaker."

Winburn and Bloom then asked for a show of support. Lynn's hand immediately went up, followed by Elliot Gerson of Travelers. Everyone else in the room quickly fell into line. Alvord, sitting next to Winburn, leaned over and said, "We want Katharine Hepburn." Gerson, on his way out of the room, said: "Charles O. Perry for the Travelers. I'll call to confirm." The project had taken flight.

By the end of the week, nine corporations officially signed up and Winburn and Bloom started to try to match them each with the artist they chose. For the next few months, the editors visited and recruited many artists in the state, almost all of whom were enthusiastic about the project. Many of them eventually reduced their commissions to gain the support of the corporations.

Winburn and Bloom often took company representatives to meet the artists. They took Gerson and his colleague Ernie Osborne to visit Perry, known for his large public sculptures, in his studio in Norwalk. On the trip to Norwalk, Gerson and Osborne said they loved the project but confessed they had no real money to spend on it, especially for a sculpture. In an earlier visit with the editors, Perry made the observation that a company that typically commissions an artist, usually for work on its grounds, "will nickel and dime the piece but then spend $60,000 on the party to unveil it."When the four visitors got to Perry's studio, he began talking about his own vision of Hartford and how a great piece of sculpture could help identify not only the city but also the great corporations with headquarters there. Gerson and Osborne began getting excited. At one point Perry said, "We should build a huge piece in the middle of the Connecticut River, a kind of eastern equivalent of the St. Louis Arch." The Travelers' visitors, bursting

Lary Bloom, editor of The Courant's Northeast magazine.

with enthusiasm, began offering their own ideas, including one that was finally adopted—putting a large Perry sculpture in the pond in Hartford's Bushnell Park.

On the trip home, Gerson and Osborne were almost giddy discussing how they might come up with the money. They agreed they could move cash from other projects to fund Perry's work, which would bring the company greater visibility and be more fun to do. Thus today, 25 years later, the 10-foot tall Perry sculpture entitled "Harmony" still adorns Bushnell Park.

A name for the project remained elusive. None of the possibilities pleased Winburn and Bloom. Masterworks? The Immortals? The Arts Legacy? Public Works? pARTners? None captured the spirit of the project. Finally, in one of their many meetings with graphics designer Peter Good of Chester, who had been working on a logo for months, Winburn and Bloom tossed out more ideas. But none were as good as Peter's, who in a constant fit of doodling on the back of an envelope, came up with it: Art For All.

By then, Winburn and Bloom had enlisted eight more outstanding artists chosen by the companies:

• Peter Blume, the Russian-born surrealist painter who lived in Sherman, Conn. At age 80, he had always worked for himself and had never been commissioned. He had just finished one of his season's paintings entitled "Autumn," an explosion of brilliant colors The painting was much too expensive—then worth at least $150,000—for his sponsoring company, Aetna. But he wanted to be part of the project. So he suggested that Aetna purchase 10 prints with its commission and distribute them in public places around Connecticut. Aetna happily complied.

• Cleve Gray, a painter renowned for his large, vividly colorful abstract compositions, who lived in Warren, Conn. He matched up with United Technologies and his painting for the project, "Cataract #2," was hung in the then new terminal at Bradley International Airport.

• Dave Brubeck, the great jazz pianist and composer who had a home in Wilton, Conn. Brubeck was commissioned by Advest, which had been overlooked and not invited to the Hartford Club breakfast. But when Chairman Anthony LaCrois heard of the project he didn't hesitate. He instantly choose Brubeck, thinking that a composition, unlike a statue, could be created over and over again—it could live anywhere at any time. Brubeck didn't disappoint. He wrote four new choral pieces for high school choruses and introduced them at a special Art For All concert at the Cigna Corp. attended by about 500 invited guests.

• Katharine Hepburn, the legendary actress who lived in the Fenwick section of Old Saybrook, Conn., when she wasn't making movies. It took Bloom, writing her dozens of letters and a possible script about her childhood years in Hartford that he put together from interviews she had given over the years, and her brother-in-law Ellsworth Grant, a frequent contributor to Northeast, to convince her. The script apparently did it—she used it as a starting point and wrote her own script for a documentary about growing up in Hartford. The video was commissioned by Connecticut National Bank and distributed to Hartford's public schools.

• Robert Cottingham, pop artist, graphic designer and photorealist who lived and worked on a farm in Newtown, Conn. He was in the process of creating 12 panels depicting railroad symbols when the Connecticut Bank and Trust Co. chose him—the perfect artist to be highlighted in the newly renovated Union Station in Hartford.

• Stevan Dohanos, artist and illustrator best known for his 125 covers for The Saturday Evening Post who lived in Westport, Conn., and was a founder of the Famous Artists School of Westport. Some of Dohanos' paintings hang in the New Britain Museum of American Art, so partnering with New Britain's Stanley Works was a natural. When it became obvious that the Stanley Works representatives were working with a very tight budget, Dohanos allowed them to pick any of his paintings other than his Post covers. During a tour of his house, they chose an apple-and-kettle still life hanging in his kitchen and agreed to his request to pay for an edition of prints that would be distributed in public places in Connecticut.

• Robert Natkin, a painter who rose to prominence in the 1970s for his work that blended Abstraction with post-Impressionist colors. He lived in Redding and was an advocate of mass production. He was commissioned by the Hartford Steam Boiler Company to do a series of posters.

• Elizabeth MacDonald, the renowned creator of ceramic paintings and sculpture who lived in Bridgewater, Conn. She was commissioned by The Hartford and her sculpture is on a sliver of land at the intersection of Farmington Avenue, Broad Street and Asylum Avenue, close to The Hartford and The Courant.

Nine world-class artists, but it wasn't enough for Winburn, who insisted that the project have 10 artists and that The Courant be the 10th sponsoring company. She made her case to Davies, who balked at first but finally relented to Winburn's persistence.

That led to one of the most dazzling projects, created by Hartford sculptor Elbert Weinberg, who though he had won the Prix de Rome and was known as the sculptor's sculptor, never had the fame of his good friend Perry. Weinberg had an idea for an enormous abstract sculpture to be placed on the grounds of the new Legislative Office Building (LOB), at Broad Street and Capitol Avenue across the street from The Courant. It would take some time to complete, with much of the work done in a Brooklyn, N.Y., foundry. Also taking some time were The Courant's negotiations with the legislative leadership to give the massive sculpture a home in the LOB's Minuteman Park.

The timing couldn't have been worse. Weinberg, who was suffering from a rare disease of the bone marrow, died before the piece could be finally constructed. Months later, his mother, then 92 years old, sat in for him at the dedication ceremony in Minuteman Park for the last piece of public art in Art for All, entitled "Pickles and Palm Trees."

Northeast magazine, under Bloom and Winburn, generated many innovations but none as remarkable as Art For All.

How You Can Embrace Innovation: The best way to ensure innovation is to encourage it in your employees. That means creating an atmosphere in which they feel free to offer their ideas and taking a chance on some of them. Remember that the more passionate people feel about their ideas the more likely they will be successful.

Hilary Schneider
former executive vice president, Yahoo! Americas

Leadership Sketch No. 6

As executive vice president of Yahoo! Americas, Hilary Schneider was responsible for the company's North American, Central American and South American business, including advertising sales, partnerships and programming. She reported directly to CEO Carol Bartz until she left the company in October 2010.

She joined the company in 2006 after holding senior leadership positions at Knight Ridder, Inc., where she was CEO of Knight Ridder Digital before moving to co-manage the company's overall newspaper and online business. Before joining Knight Ridder, Hilary was president and CEO of Red Herring Communications, overseeing Red Herring Magazine and its online and events units.

She also held several leadership positions at The Times Mirror Co., including president and CEO of Times Mirror Interactive and general manager of The Sun in Baltimore. Before that, she was vice president of corporate finance at Drexel Burnham Lambert. She earned a bachelor's degree in economics from Brown University and a M.B.A. degree from the Harvard Business School.

Hilary's key leadership tips are:

- **Build smart, passionate teams** and then set them free.
- **Feedback is a gift.** Practice giving it on a weekly basis.
- **Never be too serious.** Laughter and shared adventure is the alchemy that takes you from good teams to great teams.

CHAPTER 13:

Commit to Diversity

"Diversity has been written into the DNA of American life. Any institution that lacks a rainbow array has come to seem diminished, if not diseased."

—JOURNALIST JOE KLEIN

In 1984, the editors of *The Los Angeles Times* were not satisfied with the progress being made at hiring, retaining and promoting people of color at their newspaper or in the industry. They were trying to serve one of America's most diverse communities but had few minority staff members. The rest of the industry was no better off. It was difficult to find and recruit experienced journalists of color. Yet the editors believed it was essential to get wider voices and perspectives involved in making important coverage decisions to better serve their diverse readership. But promoting journalists of color to leadership positions required hiring a large number of them to start the process.

So the editors, with the full support of the company's top brass, convinced Times Mirror to jointly fund at a cost of about $1 million a year a special training program for people of color with little or no journalism experience. They called it MET-PRO—Minority Editorial Training Program—and recruited the first class of eight inexperienced reporters and two photographers. The graduates would join the staffs of newspapers owned by Times Mirror and populate the nation's other newsrooms.

Though it began as a one-year project, it quickly became a two-year training program. The trainees, provided a salary, free housing and utilities and medical benefits, spent the first year at *The Los Angeles Times,* starting with eight weeks of intensive classroom instruction on reporting, writing, interviewing and researching. They then spent six weeks covering the police and criminal courts beats. Next came an eight-week assignment on the staff of one of the Times' regional editions. Finally, they were advanced to one of the newspaper's four main editions to work as reporters or photographers.

In the second year, the trainees were assigned to one of the Times Mirror newspapers—*The Los Angeles Times, Newsday, The Baltimore Sun, The Hartford Courant, The Morning Call* in Allentown, Pa., or *The Stamford Advocate* and *Greenwich Time* in Connecticut. Their compensation and benefits depended upon the levels at the individual newspapers. When the trainees completed the second year successfully, they became regular staff members of the newspaper or could be hired by other newspapers across the country.

From the beginning METPRO was a stunning success. Applications averaged about 200 a year as word of the program spread. Editors at each of the Times Mirror newspapers recruited applicants at job fairs and colleges around the country and jointly selected the top candidates for interviews. When the final 10 to 12 candidates were selected, the editors then begin jockeying for the right to select their favorite candidate for the second year of training at their newspaper. Candidates who survived most of the process but didn't make the final cut were quickly hired by other papers around the country. Even candidates who were cut in the first stage found jobs at other papers.

METPRO's success spawned a second program in 1989—METPRO for copy editors. Based at *Newsday* in New York, it was modeled after the program for reporters and photographers—the first year of training at Newsday and the second year at the other Times Mirror newspapers.

In 1997, a third offshoot—METPRO.biz—was established as a special leadership training program for business executives of color outside the publishing industry. The rigorous selection process was similar to the other METPRO programs but the candidates were more experienced and often had graduate degrees. They underwent training for only six months before being assigned to Times Mirror companies. Graduates wound up not only at Times Mirror newspapers but also at the company's magazines and other businesses.

The METPRO graduates all had fascinating stories. Consider the tale of Russell Ben-Ali, who at age 37 was selected for the METPRO reporting program in 1990 while working as an administrative clerk for the United Nations. He was married and had a small child but had to leave them to join the first year of training in Los Angeles. It was difficult—he only saw his wife and child seven times that year. He was reunited with his family in the second year when he was assigned to *Newsday.* In 1991, he and another METPRO trainee, photographer Mitsu Yasukawa, were part of a team that covered a subway crash in Manhattan that left five dead and more than 200 injured and won the Pulitzer Prize for spot news in 1992.

The programs were so successful that *Fortune* magazine in July 1998 named Times Mirror No. 27 on its list of "The 50 Best Companies for Asians, Blacks and Hispanics."

In all, the three METPRO programs produced more than 300 journalists of color, many of exceptional talent and many of them women, about 75 business executives and dozens of unsuccessful candidates who were hired by other newspaper companies. Graduate Clarence Williams won a Pulitzer Prize for feature photography for *The Los Angeles Times* in 1998 for powerful images documenting the plight of young children with parents addicted to alcohol and drugs. In addition, more than two dozen METPRO graduates were part of reporting and photography teams that won Pulitzer Prizes for *The Los Angeles Times* and *Newsday* over the years.

But the success didn't last. Eventually, retention became a problem—journalists of color in the early 21st Century were leaving newspapers at twice the rate of white journalists. Shortly after 2000 when Tribune Co. acquired Times Mirror, METPRO classes started shrinking. METPRO.biz was the first to die and by 2007, all three programs had been eliminated by Tribune, whose executives thought they were too costly in difficult economic times. In addition, the newspapers' editors didn't support hiring trainees at the same time they were being asked to make significant staff reductions.

But diversity is about more than race and gender. Nat Hentoff of *The Village Voice* recalls that after he had won a major journalism award some years ago, he was told by a member of the jury that there had been strong resistance among some jurors to giving him the award. It was not because of the quality of his work, the juror said. It had more to do about concern for Hentoff's conservative attitudes toward abortion, the death penalty, affirmative action and the Second Amendment.

Committing to diversity also means hiring and promoting men and women of different ages, educational backgrounds, life experiences and political attitudes.

How You Can Commit To Diversity: As a leader, you'll discover that when you include people of color and different backgrounds in the daily discussion of issues you'll hear viewpoints you've never heard before. It doesn't take long to realize that diversity opens up a wider world and makes for better decisions. That's when you'll commit to promoting diversity.

CHAPTER 14:

Take Risks

"Behold the turtle. He makes progress
only when he sticks his neck out."

—JAMES B. CONANT, FORMER PRESIDENT OF HARVARD UNIVERSITY

Andrea Wong was always successful. When she was in high school in Sunnyvale, Calif., she ran a summer camp out of her house, with three sessions of 10 to 15 children each. She graduated from MIT and Stanford Business School but started out in television as a researcher for ABC. Within a couple of years she advanced to vice president of alternative programming, specials and late night, where she was forced to take risks.

"I got lucky at ABC," she says. "It was when reality programming took off. I developed a number of shows in the genre. I passed on 'Dancing With the Stars' twice before I agreed to broadcast it. It was a risk because no one thought ballroom dancing would work."

In 2007, Wong became CEO of Lifetime Networks and continues her successful ways today. She credits her parents for their willingness to let her fail from an early age. "I ran for class secretary in high school and lost," she says. "I tried out for the drill team and didn't make it. But I learned how to pick myself up, dust myself off and keep going. My parents never let me quit once I committed to something, either."

Not quitting and trying again are vital ingredients to taking risks. No one knows that better than Lary Bloom, for 20 years the editor of *The Hartford Courant's Northeast* magazine.

Long a fan of poetry, Bloom had the idea of throwing a poetry party. He announced it on the cover of *Northeast* one Sunday in the summer of 1986 and scheduled it for the following Wednesday at the Joseloff Gallery at the University of Hartford. Even with only three days' notice, dozens of people showed up in the rain to hear three local poets—Rennie McQuilkin, Lonnie Black and Sue Ellen Thompson—read from their work.

Bloom repeated the event the next summer with three different poets at Trinity College in Hartford but for some reason the idea disappeared for five years. In 1992, McQuilkin and Sarah Lyttle, then director of the Hill-Stead Museum in Farmington, Ct., visited Bloom and deputy *Northeast* editor Jan Winburn to see if they couldn't resurrect some kind of poetry series.

The success of developing partnerships in the Art For All project (see Chapter 12) gave Bloom and Winburn confidence that they could create a new one with the Hill-Stead. The museum was the perfect venue—it boasted a beautiful sunken garden. And they knew they could get the support of The Courant management. They presented their idea to me—a festival of poetry with Connecticut poets reading their work on four summer nights at the Hill-Stead Museum's sunken garden. The magazine would profile each of the poets 10 days before their appearance. The cost of the project seemed reasonable--$25,000 for the first year, a small sum for a newsroom with a multi-million dollar budget. The real risk was being embarrassed if few people showed up.

The timing was perfect, Bloom argued. Twenty-four hour news cycles were bringing us news of dire consequences, from Desert Storm to the latest gang warfare. But a few chosen words read by poets in the summertime would be a way to escape. We agreed, though we privately doubted many people would show up, and thus was born the Sunken Garden Poetry Festival.

The very first night proved me wrong and Bloom right. Hundreds, almost 2,000 people, flocked to the Hill-Stead, tying up traffic on a Wednesday night in Farmington. Hugh Ogden, accompanied by a bass player, read his work to the huge gathering, some who expected harmless or pointless verse. When Ogden uttered his first four-letter word, two women snapped up their lawn chairs and left in a huff.

"It was a sign of what was to come for the next several years," Bloom says, "world-class poets dealing with the most difficult issues in society—domestic abuse, the threat to the environment, oppression, war, devastating illness—yet all the while revealing the deft touch of the artist who, in a very few words, can illicit chills of recognition.

"The very first year, on a rainy night (we had to move the festivities from the garden to a museum building) something happened that made us all feel this was meant to be. The door to the back fields of the museum was left open, to let air in, and poet Sue Ellen Thompson stood at the podium in front of it. Just as she uttered the sentence 'I never saw my father naked' a bolt of lightning struck right behind her. Smoke rose from the ground. Audience members gasped. Sue Ellen took a deep breath. And then read on."

Over the years, nationally acclaimed poets—Galway Kinnell, Richard Wilbur, Stanley Kunitz, Lucille Clifton, Donald Hall, Sharon Olds, Mark Doty and James Merrill—rushed to the Hill-Stead and made it the best-attended poetry festival in the country, prompting *The New York Times* to say in a headline, "Beware of Poetry Traffic Jam."

Who would have believed that a newspaper could team up with a museum and create a festival of poetry in a small town in Connecticut that would over the years draw thousands from a dozen states? I didn't. But that's what can happen when you take a risk.

How You Can Take Risks: People are hesitant to take risks for fear that their mistakes will be punished. All too often their fears are justified. You can encourage risk-taking by compiling a record of tolerating, even celebrating, mistakes. You need to build a record of encouraging risks before most people will believe it is safe to try new approaches.

Douglas E. Zemke
former president of
Millikin University in Decatur, Ill.

Leadership Sketch No. 7

Doug Zemke retired in December 2010 after serving since 2003 as the 13th president of Millikin University. A 1966 Millikin graduate, Zemke was dean of Millikin's Tabor School of Business from 1998 to 2001 and a member of the school's Board of Trustees from 1995 to 1998.

Before that, Zemke served more than 30 years as a business executive in the telecommunications industry with such companies as Illinois Bell, AT&T and Cincinnati Bell. He retired as senior vice president of Cincinnati Bell in 1997, where he led all activities associated with the restructuring of the business from 1993 to 1995.

As Millikin's president, Zemke focused the university's energies on leadership development, revitalizing curriculum with an emphasis on developing international educational opportunities, establishing fiscal responsibility and building strong ties to Millikin alums and the Decatur community. In his time in business and at Millikin, Zemke served on the boards of dozens of civic organizations.

Zemke's key leadership tips are:

- **Don't assume you have the best answer to solve a problem just because of your position.** Listen well and value others' perspectives as you formulate the solution.

- **Treat others around you, especially your subordinates, with dignity and respect,** even if you are disappointed with their performance. The issue is their performance, not their value as human beings.

- **In building and maintaining relationships, understand the difference between a "scratch" and a "puncture."** A scratch makes a red mark and causes short temporary pain. A puncture creates a painful wound that leaves a permanent scar. In dealing with people in tense situations, be careful to only scratch them rather than puncture them.

- **Don't accept quick "shoot-from-the-hip" answers to complex issues.** If the answer was that easy, it already would have been found. Stand your ground while seeking a well thought-out answer.

CHAPTER 15:
Uphold Standards and Reward Performance

"There are two things that people want more than sex or money—recognition and praise."

—MARY KAY ASH, CEO OF MARY KAY COSMETICS

In 1970, when I was chief of the local copy desk at *The Louisville Times,* I attended a week-long seminar for copy desk chiefs and wire editors at the American Press Institute, then located at Columbia University in New York. I returned to the newspaper with many ideas to implement but none more vital than instituting annual performance evaluations of the staff.

Some newsrooms had been conducting performance evaluations for a few years, notably the newspapers owned by the Knight-Ridder Co. But most editors resisted them as being too bureaucratic and time-consuming. I, too, thought they were bureaucratic and time-consuming but believed they would be the best way to set standards and hold people accountable despite the fact that most journalists, like most intellectuals, detested any attempts to assess their performance.

So we began by defining our expectations for each newsroom position—beat reporter, general assignment reporter, copy editor, origination editor, photographer, artist, columnist, every position we had. The supervising editors, working with staff members on goals and expectations, wrote the evaluations and judged the staff member's performance against the standards.

The system was uneven, especially in the beginning. Some editors were better than others in writing evaluations and keeping a record of the staff member's achievements.

Other editors were not skilled in offering constructive criticism. Because of that, the process sometimes could be painful. Nevertheless, the paper's standards were better defined and beginning to be upheld.

The next issue that surfaced was what to do with poor performers. Dealing with them was essential if only because the staff expected the managers to weed out poor performers. Ignoring poor performers only choked staff morale. We established a standard that when a staff member received a poor performance grade new goals would be set and the supervising editor would meet with him every three months for the next year. If the staff member made progress at the end of the year, his "probation" could be lifted. If no progress was made, his probation might be extended for three months or we would ask him to leave.

From 1978 to 1994, as managing editor and editor of *The Kansas City Star and Times* and executive editor and editor of *The Hartford Courant* (two newspapers free of unions), I reviewed every evaluation written by supervising editors of every staff member to assure that the standards were being applied with some evenness. When I had questions, I met with the supervising editor and discussed them. Those sessions gave me great insight into not only the staff member being evaluated but also the editor writing the evaluation. In all those years, I reviewed about 6,500 performance evaluations. In Kansas City, we asked more than two dozen staff members to seek careers elsewhere and were sued only twice, accused of age discrimination and libel. We fought the charges in court and won each case—a jury and a judge found the Star well within its rights to uphold its standards.

Just as important as upholding standards is rewarding superior performance. The easiest way was via compensation. The best performers got the largest raises—something easy to do in a pay-for-performance system at non-union newspapers. Sometimes we gave out cash bonuses for great work. Pay raises and bonuses were fine but staff members yearned for more—they wanted recognition for superior work, the more public the better.

Detailed, thoughtful notes praising outstanding work are always more effective than "attaboys." Better yet were gifts. At *The Sun,* we gave out tickets to staff members to Oriole baseball games, sometimes in the company skybox, a special treat. In Hartford, a dinner for two at a good restaurant was often the reward for excellent work. Tickets to movies were always welcomed as were American Express certificates. At each paper we gave out Publisher's Excellence Awards to outstanding performers at quarterly employee meetings. Under CEO Mark Willes, Times Mirror also awarded outstanding performance prizes in which all the award winners and their spouses from all the companies were invited to an annual awards dinner in Los Angeles. All the costs were paid for by Times Mirror.

New professional opportunities were great rewards. An inspiring young reporter who did excellent work might get his or her first national or overseas assignment. In Kansas City and Hartford, we set up rotations on the copy desk—a reporter would get the opportunity to work on the desk three months and a copy editor would replace the reporter. Most participants loved the experience.

Teaching sabbaticals also were a favorite. At the Star and Times, I set up an exchange system with the journalism schools at the University of Kansas and the University of Missouri. We provided a mid-career journalist to teach courses at the university for one semester and the university provided a journalism professor to work at the newspaper. We did the same at The

Courant with the University of Connecticut. Dozens of journalists applied for the program, with the university selecting the final candidate.

Perhaps the greatest reward program of all was started in 1996 by Willes when the company announced it would reward exceptional performance in all the companies with the Times Mirror Stock Recognition Award. Each company would nominate outstanding achievers for grants of up to 2,500 stock options. During the first year, 11 Courant employees from various department won performance options. We highlighted their achievements in a brochure passed out to all employees. Hundreds of employees at Times Mirror companies won stock option grants before the program died in 2000 with the merger of Times Mirror and Tribune Co.

How You Can Uphold Standards And Reward Performance:
One of the best ways to uphold standards is to reward exceptional performance. Even without much of a budget for rewards, small treats work wonders and are inexpensive. Tickets to movies, stage plays, sporting events and music concerts as well as a dinner for two at a good restaurant will send the message that the quality bar has been elevated and outstanding work is appreciated.

CHAPTER 16:

Be Tenacious

"Many of life's failures are people who did not realize how close they came to success when they gave up."

—THOMAS EDISON

The final round of professional golf's greatest tournament, the U. S. Open, always falls on Father's Day, with the winners frequently mentioning lessons learned from their fathers. Hale Irwin was no exception. One of the lessons his Dad had taught him was "don't start something you can't finish." Those words were haunting Irwin after shooting a 74 in the opening round in the Florida Citrus Open in Orlando in 1976. He was tired.

"I had played a lot that year," Irwin says. "I told an official I wanted to withdraw, went in to clean out my locker and it felt… wrong. I could hear my Dad: 'Don't do it.' I kept playing and figured if I missed the cut, at least I hadn't quit. I shot a second round 64, then two 66's on the weekend and won a four-hole playoff. I went from withdrawing to winning. That put a nail in the quit coffin."

Hartford Courant reporter Steve Grant must have used the same hammer. Early in 1988, Grant wrote a long memo to me and other editors proposing a new beat. He cited remarks I had

Steve Grant of The Hartford Courant beginning his adventure canoeing the Connecticut River in Vermont in 1991.
Photo by Michael McAndrews, courtesy of The Hartford Courant

previously made in the newsroom about constantly reviewing what we covered and how we did it.

Grant, an outstanding reporter whose modesty belies his exceptional talent, proposed that he cover his environment beat in a new way. Instead of first focusing on the regulatory side of environmental protection—air, water, hazardous waste and such—he suggested writing from the perspective of some of the things people wanted to protect, such as rivers, mountains, plants and animals. The idea was to emphasize coverage of the natural sciences and demonstrate in various ways why anyone should care about the Connecticut River or an old, undisturbed forest or an endangered species.

Grant struck a nerve; within a couple of days we approved his idea and he was off to the wilderness. But it was on campuses where he discovered a gold mine of terrific stories that were all but totally overlooked by American newspapers. He met frequently with the heads of university biology departments and deans of forestry schools to discover what research they were conducting. Each time he visited a school he returned with great story ideas, many of which wound up on Page One.

Like the story of the tiny frogs.

He spent time with a University of Connecticut professor who studied how tiny frogs like spring peepers can peep for so many hours in the spring without exhausting themselves. His research, focusing on a tiny muscle, was shedding light on muscle physiology that had implications for humans.

Readers loved it. Both the paper and Grant got lots of positive feedback on these kinds of stories.

For years Grant had wanted to canoe the entire length of the Connecticut River, from its source 300 yards south of the Canadian border to its mouth in Long Island Sound. But his story proposals fell on deaf ears.

One evening early in 1991, the deputy managing editor, Claude Albert, and Grant were chatting in the newsroom as I wandered by. "What crazy story ideas are you pitching now?" I asked Grant. Albert interjected: "Don't get him started or he'll bring up his Connecticut River idea."

"What's that?" I asked. "I've suggested that I canoe the entire Connecticut River and write about it," Grant replied.

"You could do that?' I asked. "How long would it take?"

"About a month," Grant estimated.

I asked him to give us a memo outlining his plan. He did the next day and his editor, Pam Luecke, and I signed off on the project that very day, with these instructions: "Take as long as it takes to do it right, write it well, be careful and don't get hurt."

Grant's tenacity had paid off. He spent several weeks preparing for the trip. Much of his time was taken up with research, talking to various experts throughout the four Connecticut River states—New Hampshire, Vermont, Massachusetts and Connecticut. He interviewed geologists, botanists, foresters, farmers, land-use experts, environmental groups, state fisheries biologists and water quality engineers. The Courant outfitted him with the latest in equipment, including cooking gear he used so often on the trip that the paper reprinted his favorite recipes for food he prepared along the river—Maplemont Farm Chicken Stew, Camper's Baking Powder Biscuits and Littleton Spider Corn Cakes.

He started the journey on May 29, 1991 at the source of the Connecticut in Pittsburg, N. H., a town of a few hundred people living in several hundred square miles of forests, lakes and streams.

On some days he was accompanied by Michael McAndrews, a Courant photographer who documented the 410-mile journey to Long Island Sound.

But mostly Grant was by himself, camping out along the banks and occasionally staying with residents living along the river. He carried a laptop computer that worked on batteries and electricity. To file stories, he coupled his computer to a telephone—maybe a pay telephone in a nearby town one day or a farmhouse phone on another day—and pressed a key that sent them into The Courant's computer. Once in a while, he tried to use his cell phone, a crude device that rarely worked, to send his stories.

Grant wrote three articles a week, accompanied by McAndrews' photographs, describing his adventure and the sights, sounds and smells of the Connecticut River. He described the people he met, the flora and fauna he encountered and the ecology dangers that lurked. He wrote about portaging around 17 dams with not just his 16-foot canoe but with all his gear and provisions, ranging from dozens of vegetables, dried fruits, pasta and rice to coffee, cornmeal, crackers and a half-dozen herbs.

Readers couldn't get enough.

They called The Courant by the dozens each time a story appeared, praising the series. A Hartford radio station, WTIC-AM, arranged to interview Grant a few times along the way. It wasn't easy, because cell phone service, then in its infancy, was so spotty.

"We worked out a deal where I called the station at a designated time," Grant says. "I think it was 7 a.m. I had to call from a pay phone because I did not have cell service. One time, I remember leaving a campsite and paddling from 5:30 a.m. to 6:30 a.m. so I could get to a pay phone in Bellows Falls, Vt. Once I was on the line with WTIC they would wait until the news and traffic reports were done and then go to a live interview with me."

A reporter from the National Public Radio affiliate in Western Massachusetts met Grant on the river one day. She joined him in the canoe for a few hours and taped their conversation, which later became short on-the-air features throughout the journey.

The newspaper and radio coverage generated excitement all along the Connecticut. On many days, boating enthusiasts met

Photo by Michael McAndrews, courtesy The Hartford Courant

Steve Grant of The Hartford Courant canoeing into Long Island Sound from the Connecticut River.

Grant on the river and paddled with him, some for a few miles and others for nearly an entire day. Large crowds gathered on the riverbanks in Springfield, Mass., and Hartford to greet him.

On the 33rd day, June 30, 1991, Grant was about five miles from Old Saybrook, Conn., and the end of his journey when he spotted a couple of hundred people waving at him, clapping from the shoreline. Others were tooting their boat horns. People stopped to take pictures and film him with home video cameras.

About a mile before Saybrook Point, Grant was met by a group of paddlers that included his wife Susan, his sister and brother-in-law, Susan and Joseph Balsis, a friend, Bill Bender, and several members of the Connecticut River Watershed

Council and the state Department of Environmental Protection. Tucked inside two of the canoes were his daughter Allison, age 8, and son Scott, age 4.

About 45 minutes later, they pulled into Saybrook Point, where nearly 500 people greeted him. There were ceremonies—Grant drinking champagne and then being doused with a bottle of it, speeches lauding his journey and stories and remarks by the canoeist himself. And finally the crowd started breaking up.

But Grant wasn't finished. Only his family and some friends remained. The actual end of the river was still three-quarters of a mile south. Grant quietly put his canoe back into the water and hopped in, along with his brother-in-law. In his last story, he described in his usual modest way the actual end of the journey.

"The wind was with us now, the tide going out. We plowed through the water, smacking against sturdy wakes and waves.

"In minutes—maybe 15 minutes—we reached Lynde Point, and the breakwater that marks the beginning of Long Island Sound.

"We pulled ashore. There was no ceremony now. The few of us left just shook hands. It was getting cool. I should have been tired, but I felt fresh.

"A little while later, I drove off with my battered canoe on top of my car."

How You Can Be Tenacious: Too often people give up on their dreams, even small ones, when obstacles surface. But most successful people keep plugging away, even at the risk of being considered a pest, until they reach their goal. Reading about people who have overcome adversity can inspire you to stay the course, no matter how big the obstacle.

Dr. Carla D. Hayden
executive director of the
Enoch Pratt Free Library in Baltimore

Leadership Sketch No. 8

D r. Carla D. Hayden has been head of Baltimore's Enoch Pratt Free Library since 1993. Before that she was the first deputy commissioner and chief librarian at the Chicago Public Library, an assistant professor in the School of Library and Information Science at the University of Pittsburgh and library services coordinator at the Museum of Science and Industry in Chicago.

She is an active member of the American Library Association and was president of the organization in 2003-04. She serves on several boards of civic organizations, including the Maryland African-American Museum Corp. and Baltimore Leadership School for Young Women. In June 2010, the Senate approved her nomination by President Obama to the board of the Institute of Museums and Library Services.

Dr. Hayden has won many awards over the years, including being named one of the Women of the Year by Ms. Magazine in 2003 and Librarian of the Year by Library Journal in 1995. She earned a bachelor's degree in 1973 from Roosevelt

University and her master's and doctor's degrees from the Graduate Library School at the University of Chicago.

Dr. Hayden's key leadership tips are:

- **Serve first, then lead.** Taking ownership and being involved inspires and motivates.

- **Set a clear mission, goal or philosophy.** This allows everyone to be connected on a certain goal and helps in assessing the organization's character in terms of ethics and performance.

- **Be open to what people have to offer.**

CHAPTER 17:
The Enemies of Leadership

*"Our greatest foes, and whom we must
chiefly combat, are within."*

—MIGUEL DE CERVANTES, NOVELIST AND POET

The enemies of leadership are many, but as Cervantes and Pogo suggest, they are mostly us. Here are just a few:

• **Micromanagment.** This might be the Number One enemy of leadership. Every company has dozens, even hundreds, of micromanagers. They are control freaks, unable to delegate authority to their subordinates. As a result, they rob people's ability to learn how to make decisions and to learn from making their own mistakes.

• **Indecisiveness.** This is the first cousin of Micromanagement. The leader becomes so overwhelmed by detail that it becomes difficult to make a decision, resulting in Decision Gridlock, which undercuts his authority. As the copy desk chief for staff-produced stories at *The Louisville Times,* I worked for a news editor, Jack Carey, who frequently argued that a bad decision is better than no decision. He was right. As the designer of the inside pages of the newspaper, Carey could not act until the Page One editor decided on which stories he would use for the front page. The later the Page One editor acted, the more Carey was stifled in making his decisions and the more chances increased that edition deadlines would be missed, resulting in papers being delivered late.

• **Importantitis.** This disease of out-of-control egos has wrecked many a career. One of the most noteworthy to suffer its wounds was Leonard Bernstein, who captivated Broadway in 1957 with the great musical "West Side Story." But for the next 33 years until his death in 1990 he floundered, unable to compose anything worthy of any note. His collaborator on "West Side Story," Stephen Sondheim, told Meryle Secrest, who wrote biographies of both men, that Bernstein developed "a bad case of importantitis." The disease inflicts many politicians, says Jenny Sanford, the former wife of South Carolina Gov. Mark Sanford, who admitted to a year-long affair with an Argentine divorcee. "Politicians become disconnected from the way everyone else lives," she says. "They'll say they need something, and 10 people want to give it to them. It's an ego boost, and it's easy to drink your own Kool-Aid." When importantitis strikes, victims should immediately recite Emily Dickinson's famous poem, "I'm Nobody! Who are you?"

• **Bad Execution.** According to *Fortune Magazine,* most unsuccessful CEOs stumble because of one key shortcoming: bad execution. It doesn't matter how good the strategic plan is; if it's poorly executed and generates weak results the CEO's future is likely to be in jeopardy. The same is true for most leaders. Words and charm can only take you so far. Results are required for advancement.

• **Missing In Action.** I knew of a newspaper publisher who never seemed to be on the job and therefore had a difficult time ever fashioning an effective executive team. He frequently was out of town at one of his two homes elsewhere in the country and in addition often on vacation—up to eight or ten weeks a year. At least that's what his key executives thought. When he was at the paper, he was not often seen by employees. In the end, he was ineffective because he was too often missing in action.

• **Nostalgia.** The longing for the "good old days," carried to extremes, is a dangerous enemy of leadership. At *The Sun,* several veteran employees were so enamored with the past that they seemed frozen in time and unable to cope with the present. Years after the professional football team, the Colts, left Baltimore for Indianapolis, the nostalgia corps was still unable to accept the new team, the Ravens. When nostalgia strikes, remember that some time in the future "today" will be someone's "good old days."

• **Poor Hiring.** Some leaders ultimately fail because they surround themselves with mediocre people, fearful that talented subordinates would be threatening to them. When asked what makes for a good manager, baseball great Yogi Berra replied: "Good players." Hire the best people you can find, give them real authority and get out of their way.

Acknowledgements

I must first recognize and salute the eight leaders who offered excellent tips in the Leadership Sketches: Mary Junck, Freeman Hrabowski, Marty Petty, Mike Mulvain, John Carroll, Hilary Schneider, Doug Zemke and Carla Hayden.

I am also indebted to Stan Slusher, former assistant managing editor of *The Courier-Journal,* who served as an outstanding chief editor of the manuscript.

Also making valuable contributions were present or former staff members of four newspapers:

From *The Kansas City Star and Times:* David Zeeck, Darryl Levings, Rick Alm, Roy Wenzl, Monroe Dodd and Steve Shirk.

From *The Hartford Courant:* Lary Bloom, Bruce DeSilva, Marty Petty, Lou Golden, David Fink, Elaine Kramer, Steve Grant, Ed Mahony, Irving Kravsow, Henry Scott, Matt Poland, Rosa Ciccio, Michael McAndrews, John Scanlan and John Zakarian.

From *The Sun* in Baltimore: John Carroll, Tom Linthicum, Luwanda Jenkins, John Patinella and Rich Goldstein.

From *The Los Angeles Times:* Richard Kipling.

I'm also grateful for the excellent advice of literary agent David Groff and Doug Weaver, publisher of Kansas City Star Books, who also guided me through the process of producing a book. And many thanks to designer Amy Robertson, whose work turned a plain manuscript into a shining gem.

Finally, I want to recognize two former high school coaches in Durand, Ill., Sid Felder and Milt Truesdale, who taught me many of the book's leadership principles long before I ever entered a workplace.

Notes

Chapter 1: Share Power

13-14. "The CEO of Merrill Lynch..." through "In addition, O'Neal was a flawed communicator..." *The Wall Street Journal,* Oct. 29, 2007.

14. "The really good people...they want a chance to do it." *The New York Times,* Jan. 3, 2010.

15. "...Rahm Emanuel...believes the more someone uses power the more power he accumulates." *The New York Times,* Aug. 16, 2009.

15-23. The account of the Hartford Leadership Model is based on my notes and documents and those of former Hartford Courant staff members Marty Petty, Elaine Kramer, John Zakarian, David Fink and Lou Golden.

Chapter 2: Pursue Excellence

27. "Another great believer in high quality content..."
     The Wall Street Journal, May 6, 2009.

27. "In 1988, the provost at UMBC, Dr. Freeman
     Hrabowski...." UMBC.edu.

28. "Since 1993, the Myerhoff Scholarship Program...."
     UMBC.edu.

28. "Dr. Hrabowski...was named in 2009 by Time
     Magazine...." *The Sun,* Aug. 20, 2009.

Chapter 3: Include Employees

33. "A survey done more than a decade ago..." *The Wall
     Street Journal,* (date unknown).

Chapter 4: Respect People

39. "When asked how he keeps more than 400 employees
     focused...." *Time Magazine,* (date unknown).

39. "Greg Brenneman, former CEO of Quiznos and Burger
     Queen...." *New York Times,* March 15, 2009.

Chapter 5: Create Teamwork

45. "A great example is the Oklahoma Thunder of the
     NBA...and a spot in the playoffs." *USA Today,* April 16,
     2010.

46-55.   The account of the 1981 coverage of the Crown Center
         Hyatt Regency disaster is based on my notes and
         records at the time and the email memos of *Kansas
         City Star and Times* journalists David Zeeck, Darryl
         Levings, Ric Alm, Roy Wenzl, Monroe Dodd and Steve
         Shirk.

Chapter 6: Become an Agent of Change

57.   "When Drew Gilpin Faust...early on she encountered
         friction and resistance to change." *New York Times,*
         Nov. 1, 2009.

Chapter 7: Excel as an Apostle of Hope

65-68. The account of Reading By 9 is based on my notes
       and documents and those of former Sun editor John
       Carroll and former Sun marketing executive Luwanda
       Jenkins.

Chapter 8: Be a Slave to Integrity

71.   "Robert Mazzuca, chief executive of the Boy Scouts
         of America...you're not a good leader no matter how
         charismatic." *USA Today,* July 21, 2008.

Chapter 9: Communicate, Communicate, Communicate

78.   "Whether you have a really small team...the same
         words mean different things to different people." Susan
         Docherty, leader of U.S. sales, service and market team
         at General Motors, *New York Times,* Feb. 7, 2010.

78.   "Many managers overestimate...less that 5 per cent
         thought they needed to improve." *The Wall Street
         Journal,* Nov. 1, 2010.

78-80.   The Abilene Paradox, by Dr. Jerry B. Harvey, is
         reprinted with permission of Dr. Harvey, Lexington
         Books and the American Management Association.

Chapter 10: Teach and Coach

81.   "When Chief Executive magazine...I'd sooner own
         a fish farm than be reliant on catching a few fish."
         George Buckley, CEO of 3M, *USA Today,* May 18,
         2009.

82-88.   The account of the writing coach years at *The
         Hartford Courant* relies on my notes and records and
         those of journalist and author Bruce DeSilva.

Chapter 11: Listen, Really Listen

93.   "William Mitchell...fortunately, he learned his lessons
         well and is now CEO of Arrow Electronics." *New York
         Times,* Nov. 11, 2007.

93-94.   "Another CEO, Randy Benard...It is my job to make
         sure I can understand all their concerns, while at the
         same time do what is right." *USA Today,* May 11, 2010.

94.   "Gary McCullough, president...and on that day, we
         would have followed that general anywhere." *New York
         Times,* Aug. 9, 2009.

Chapter 12: Embrace Innovation

95-102. The account of the Art for All project of *The Harford
         Courant* comes from my notes and records, from the
         email exchange about the project with editor Lary
         Bloom and from *Northeast* magazine, Sept. 27, 1987.

Chapter 13: Commit to Diversity

107-110. The account of METPRO comes from my notes and records and those of Richard Kipling, a former *The Los Angeles Times* editor and former director of METPRO, and Tom Linthicum, a former editor at *The Sun*.

110.　"Nat Hentoff of *The Village Voice* recalls…" *Editor & Publisher,* Jan. 7, 2002.

Chapter 14: Take Risks

111-112. "Andrea Wong…my parents never let me quit once I committed to something, either." *New York Times,* Aug. 30, 2009.

112-113. The account of *The Hartford Courant's* Sunken Garden Poetry Festival comes from my notes and records and from those of editor Lary Bloom.

Chapter 16: Be Tenacious

123.　"Hale Irwin was no exception…that put the nail in the quit coffin." *Golf Magazine,* June 2010.

123-129. The account of Steve Grant's expedition on the Connecticut River came from my notes and records, Grant's notes and recollections and a special reprint of his stories filed while on the journey and published by *The Hartford Courant* in August 1991.

Chapter 17: The Enemies of Leadership

134.　"IMPORTANTITIS. This disease…that Bernstein developed 'a bad case of importantitis.'" Terry Teachout column, *The Wall Street Journal.*

134. "Politicians become disconnected...it's easy to drink your own Kool-Aid." *The Island Packet,* Aug. 18, 2009.

134. "BAD EXECUTION. According to Fortune Magazine, most unsuccessful CEOs..." *Fortune Magazine,* June 21, 1999.

About the Author

Mike Waller started his newspaper career in 1961 as a sports clerk at *The Decatur Herald.* After graduating from Millikin University in Decatur, Ill., in 1963, he served for the next 15 years as a reporter and editor at *The Herald, The Cleveland Plain Dealer* and *The Courier-Journal* and *Louisville Times,* where he rose to assistant managing editor and executive sports editor. In 1978, he joined the staff of *The Kansas City Star* and become the only editor in The Star's history to serve in the top three newsroom positions: managing editor of The Star, managing editor of *The Kansas City Times* and editor of *The Kansas City Star and Times.*

Waller was named executive editor of *The Hartford Courant* in 1986, became The Courant's editor in 1990 and was appointed publisher and CEO of The Courant in 1994. Three years later he was named publisher and CEO of *The Sun* in Baltimore and senior vice president of the Times Mirror Co. During his 41-year career, he worked for newspapers that won dozens of national journalism awards, including eight Pulitzer Prizes. He retired at the end of 2002 and he and his wife Donna now live on Hilton Head Island, SC. He has written one other book, *Durand's Marvelous Merchants: A Tale of Small-Town Life and Big-Time Softball,* which is available at Amazon.com, TheKansasCityStore.com and Kansas City Store retail outlets.

9070208R0

Made in the USA
Lexington, KY
26 March 2011